Village Walks
in
EAST SUSSEX

Village Walks
in
EAST SUSSEX

Ben Perkins

COUNTRYSIDE BOOKS
NEWBURY, BERKSHIRE

First published 1998
© Ben Perkins 1998

COUNTRYSIDE BOOKS
3 Catherine Road
Newbury, Berkshire

ISBN 1 85306 505 6

Designed by Graham Whiteman
Photographs and maps by the author
Illustrations by Trevor Yorke

Front cover photo of Jevington
taken by Richard Reed

Produced through MRM Associates Ltd., Reading
Printed by J. W. Arrowsmith Ltd., Bristol

Contents

AREA MAP SHOWING LOCATION OF THE WALKS

Publisher's Note

We hope that you obtain considerable enjoyment from this book; great care has been taken in its preparation. Although at the time of publication all routes followed public rights of way or permitted paths, diversion orders can be made and permissions withdrawn.

We cannot of course be held responsible for such diversion orders and any inaccuracies in the text which result from these or any other changes to the routes nor any damage which might result from walkers trespassing on private property. We are anxious though that all details covering the walks are kept up to date and would therefore welcome information from readers which would be relevant to future editions.

Introduction

We all have our own idea of the perfect English village, or at least the ingredients which, when mixed and matched, combine to achieve our ideal. Such well loved features might include a wisteria-clad pub facing the village green and cricket ground, houses built harmoniously with local materials, quiet traffic-free lanes, a village pump, duck pond and painted ornamental sign, a small unspoilt church (preferably kept unlocked). These provide the surface picture. Equally important are the less obvious attributes such as a viable village shop, a bus service to and from the local town, the right balance of homes for local residents and holiday visitors, all of which can make the difference between a stagnant backwater and a thriving rural community. Many of the villages selected for inclusion in this book achieve a remarkably high score using these criteria.

Of equal importance when making the difficult choice of which villages to include in this book has been the quality of the surrounding countryside. East Sussex embraces parts of two designated Areas of Outstanding Natural Beauty. To the south of the county the chalk hills of the South Downs extend from the cliffs to the west of Eastbourne until they cross the county boundary to the north of Brighton (Walks 4, 5, 7, 10 and 11). To the north, spreading over into the neighbouring county of Kent, lies the extensive and surprisingly remote area of the High Weald. This is a landscape of well wooded sandy ridges (Walks 6, 9, 12, 13, 14, 16, 17 and 19). Dividing these areas are the intensively farmed valleys formed by three rivers, the Ouse, the Cuckmere

and the Eastern Rother (Walks 2, 3, 15, 18 and 20), and the clay of the Low Weald which can be very muddy underfoot during the winter months (Walks 1 and 8).

Most of the villages have reasonable car parking facilities but the available space can fill up rapidly, particularly during summer weekends. If you have to park by the roadside, make sure you do so with minimum inconvenience to residents. All but one of the walks start and finish in the featured village. For Walk 15 from Wartling where there is no room to park in the centre of the village an alternative starting point is provided. The walks have been designed mainly to explore the countryside around the village, but all can be directly linked with a tour of the village itself. When choosing a route, I have also attempted to complement rather than duplicate the walks described in the companion series of *Pub Walks* and *Walks for Motorists* published by Countryside Books.

The walks all follow designated rights of way or paths where public access is permitted and most are well signed. In the more remote areas, some care in route finding is required particularly during late summer when some paths may be obscured by growing crops or lush summer growth of nettles and brambles etc.

Before attempting any of the walks, I would strongly recommend arming yourself with an OS map. The 1:50,000 Landranger series should be adequate when used in conjunction with the route description and sketch map, but you might like to consider the excellent new Explorer series of maps, each of which combine two or three sheets from the old 1:25,000 Pathfinder series and represent excellent value for money.

Between them, the villages featured in this book demonstrate a remarkable diversity of character. All are within easy reach of other attractions, listed with each walk under 'Places of Interest'. During a summer preparing this book, I feel as if I have explored almost every corner of this rich county. In following these 20 walks, I hope you will enjoy the experience as much as I have.

Ben Perkins

DITCHLING

Length: 4½ miles

Getting there: Ditchling lies on the intersection of the B2116 Hassocks to Lewes road and the B2112 between Brighton and Haywards Heath.	**Parking:** The village car park is tucked behind the village hall a few yards to the east of the crossroads at the centre of the village.	**Maps:** OS Landranger - Brighton and the Downs 198 or OS Explorer - South Downs Way, Steyning to Newhaven 17 (GR 326151).

Ditchling stands on a low greensand hillock, overlooked by Ditchling Beacon, which at 814 feet is one of the highest points on the South Downs. During the summer months the village is at times almost overwhelmed by cars, jamming the narrow High Street where, for some inexplicable reason, there are no parking restrictions so this is a place best enjoyed out of season. The finest houses line the High Street or are grouped round the cruciform church with its characteristic pyramidal 'Sussex Cap' standing on a mound overlooking the village green. Opposite the church is Wing's Place, a remarkable 16th century mansion of brick and half timbering, one of several originally given by Henry VIII to his divorced wife,

There are three pubs, all serving food, within a few yards of the village centre. The Bull, beside the crossroads, is open all day and provides the most extensive menu (Tel: 01273 843147). The Sandrock Inn to the north along the High Street offers a simpler choice of straightforward pub food (Tel: 01273 842777). The White Horse, along East Street, is a popular 'local' freehouse, offering Harveys beer from Lewes and several guest beers as well as good basic 'pub grub', plus several vegetarian dishes (Tel: 01273 842006).

Anne of Cleves. Note the striking gables and an external flight of steps built to provide access to the first floor.

For the walk, (which includes sweeping views of the downland escarpment), we turn our back on the well worn routes up on to the Downs to follow field paths and tracks to the north of the village, reaching the southern edge of Ditchling Common. This 200 acre area is designated as a Country Park, where it is possible to roam freely and which offers possibilities for an extension of the walk if time and energy permit.

THE WALK

❶ From the crossroads in the centre of the village, start the walk westwards along the B2116, signposted to Hassocks, passing the church on your right and Wing's Place on your left. After a few more yards, turn right along Lodge Hill Lane, past the village green and pond.

Where the lane veers left, go forward through a squeeze stile and up on to the low summit of Lodge Hill, a public open space

Ditchling church.

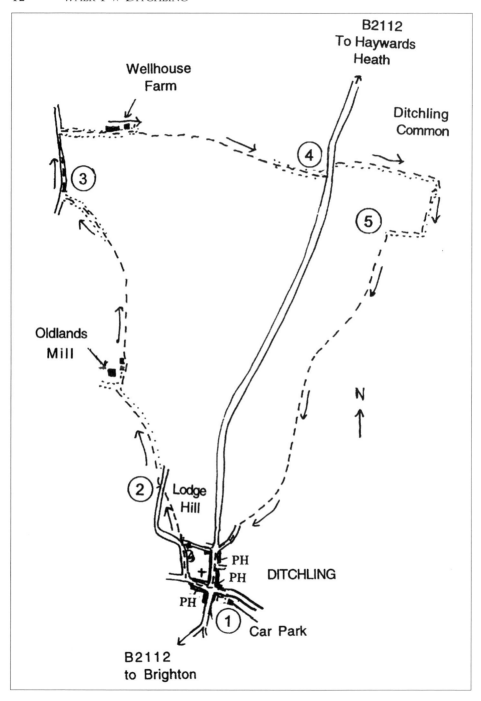

B2112
To Haywards
Heath

Wellhouse
Farm

Ditchling
Common

④

③

⑤

Oldlands
Mill

N
↑

② Lodge
Hill

PH
✝ PH   DITCHLING
PH

①
Car Park

B2112
to Brighton

which provides a fine viewpoint overlooking the village with Ditchling Beacon in the background. Veer slightly left across a grassy plateau to rejoin the lane through another squeeze stile and turn right.

❷ After 50 yards, go left over a stile and bear right along the brim of a grassy bank with a fence on your right and another wide sweeping view southwards and westwards to the Downs with the twin windmills of Jack and Jill clearly identifiable. In the field corner a short path takes you out to join a drive opposite the skeletal remains of Oldlands Mill, currently under restoration.

Turn right here on a track which skirts to the right of a house and garden. Ignore a right fork, continue past more buildings to

PLACES of INTEREST

The small but enterprising **Ditchling Museum** occupies an old school building next to the village green and houses a variety of exhibits related to the history of Sussex, plus a reconstruction of a Victorian cottage parlour and a gallery where you can see the work of local artists. During the summer months the museum offers a series of special exhibitions dealing with a variety of subjects. It is open from 1st April to 31st October on weekdays between 10.30 am and 5 pm and Sundays from 2 pm to 5 pm. Winter opening is restricted to weekends and bank holidays (Tel: 01273 844744).

go through another squeeze stile and enter a narrow fenced path which may be overgrown in places. Join a more substantial bridleway and bear left along it. The path becomes a roughly metalled drive which takes you out to a road.

The village pond at Ditchling.

❸ Turn right and follow this busy road with care as there is no verge. After about 300 yards, turn right along the roughly metalled Wellhouse Lane. After ¼ mile, opposite the farm entrance to Wellhouse Farm, go ahead on a grassy path which heads east, becoming a fenced track.

❹ About 30 yards short of the B2112, fork left on a short path through scrub to join the road. Cross the road, go left for 20 yards, then right over a stile on to Ditchling Common. Go forward along the southern edge of the common, walking parallel to power lines. In the corner go right over a stile and, after 10 yards, right over a second stile and then left to head south, with a fence on your left. Walk through scrub and then along the left-hand edge of two fields until waymarks direct you to the right along the field edge. In the field corner, go left over a stile and footbridge and ahead between fences.

❺ A well signed path now heads south once more, passing through a deer enclosure. At a T-junction of mown paths, go left through a gap in a hedge and immediately right for 30 yards to a stile. Go ahead, skirting to the left of a large garden, forward across the meadow beyond and on along a headland track.

Where the track bears right, go ahead over a stile beside a gate. After 40 yards go right over a stile and then veer half-left to the next stile. Go forward along a field edge for 30 yards and then, at a three-armed footpath sign, turn right. Go over a stile in front of stables and on to another stile in the left-hand corner of a paddock. From here an enclosed path takes you back via an access drive to Ditchling High Street. Turn left back to the start.

BARCOMBE

Length: 5 miles

Getting there: From the A275 Lewes to East Grinstead road about 3 miles north of Lewes, fork right by the Rainbow Inn, signposted to Barcombe. After a mile, turn right for another mile into Barcombe village (marked as Barcombe Cross on OS maps). Alternatively, you can approach the village from the A26 Lewes to Uckfield road, via Barcombe Mills.

Parking: A small car park is signposted from the High Street. Alternative car park (summer months only) at Barcombe Mills, just off the route about half-way round the circuit at GR 435147.

Maps: OS Landranger - Brighton and Worthing 198 or OS Explorer - South Downs Way, Steyning to Newhaven 17 (GR 420158).

On Ordnance Survey maps you will find three Barcombes. The main village, where the walk starts, is labelled Barcombe Cross, though the village sign calls it Barcombe. On the map, Barcombe is indicated less than a mile to the south and was the original settlement until most of its inhabitants were killed by the plague. It now consists of a handful of houses and a farm clustered round the church and what was the village pond. Sadly, the pond has now been incorporated into a private

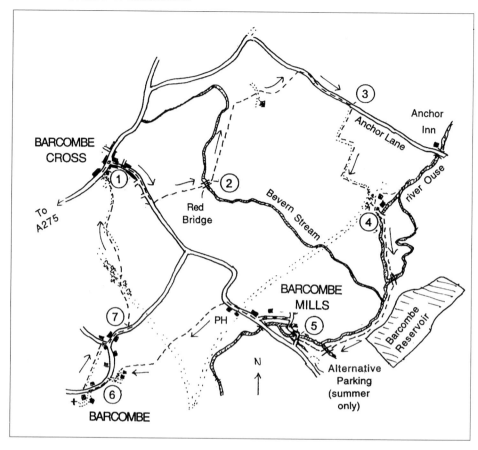

garden and is shielded from public view by a high hedge. The church, incorporating fragments dating back to the 11th century, is well worth a visit. It boasts a striking engraved glass screen, erected in 1971. A little to the east is Barcombe Mills, a delectable spot where the river Ouse splits to flow over weirs and fish ladders and through a series of mill ponds and sluices. The mill, which once stood over the main river, was destroyed by fire in 1939.

This delightful walk visits all three of these settlements. From Barcombe Cross the route follows the Bevern stream for a short distance before climbing a low eminence and descending into the main Ouse valley. After a pleasant stroll along the river bank to Barcombe Mills, field paths take us to Barcombe church and back to the start.

THE WALK

❶ From the entrance to the car park turn right and head north along the High Street. At a mini-roundabout turn right, signposted to Barcombe Mills and Ringmer. After just under 400 yards, turn left over a stile beside a gate. Follow a clear track

FOOD and DRINK

The Royal Oak pub at Barcombe Cross is a good old fashioned 'local' with an adjacent skittle alley (Tel: 01273 400418). The Angler's Rest at Barcombe Mills offers a wide variety of food and good beer (Tel: 01273 400270). The Anchor Inn, with a restaurant, is about ¼ mile off the route and can be reached either along the river bank from point 4 or via Anchor Lane from point 3 (Tel: 01273 400414). Rowing boats are available for hire and can be taken upstream to Isfield.

Next door to the Angler's Rest, the old Barcombe Mills station site has been converted to a shop, tea rooms and restaurant where you can enjoy a snack or more substantial meal seated at tables beneath the old station platform canopy.

down along the edge of two fields and across a low lying meadow to a footbridge beside a small weir (Red Bridge).

❷ Beyond the bridge, turn left for 50 yards to cross a stile and continue in the same direction with a fence on your right at first and then through a long field. At the far end, where you have a choice of two gates ahead, go through the one on the right and then bear half-right up across a field to a stile. Cross a drive to a second stile, then walk along the left-hand edge of a field to a third stile after which you should veer half-

The thatched round house and barn near Barcombe church.

left with a hedge on your left and a young plantation of trees to your right. Although only 95 ft above sea level this is the highest point on the walk with a good view across the Ouse valley. In the field corner go over a stile and turn right along the narrow Anchor Lane.

❸ After a little over ¼ mile go over a stile hidden in the hedge on your right, which is easily missed. Follow a headland path round two sides of the first field, go through a gap into a second field and immediately turn right with a hedge on your right. Once again walk round two sides of the field but about 50 yards along the second side, sidestep to the right through a gap in the hedge on your right and resume your previous direction on the other side of the hedge which will now be on your left. In the field corner follow the headland round to the right for 30 yards and then go left over a stile and through a small copse.

❹ On reaching the track bed of an old railway, turn left for 10 yards, then right over a stile and along a path laid with concrete slabs which takes you out to join a metalled farm drive. Bear right along this drive and shortly, just past a barn on your left, go left across a wide bridge over the river Ouse. On the other side of the river turn right and follow a pleasant well trodden path along the river bank for almost ½ mile to Barcombe Mills.

Barcombe church.

❺ At a lane, turn right over an ivy covered bridge. Follow this lane as it winds between mill ponds and sluices and past the old toll house where a list of the charges imposed until as recently as 1939 is displayed. At a junction, turn left and follow the lane out to join a road. Bear right along the road past the old Barcombe Mills station, now a restaurant, and the Angler's Rest. About 100 yards past the pub, go left over a stile where you have a choice of signed paths. Follow the lower, left-hand edge of two fields with stiles between them. A lavishly waymarked path then crosses three more small fields. Go over the old railway and ahead across a field where a path should be defined through any growing crop. In the next field veer half-right aiming just to the right of a house with red tile-hung walls. An enclosed path passes to the right of this house and out via the drive from the house to a T-junction with another drive. Turn right for 50 yards out to join a lane.

❻ Bear left along this lane. The church is accessible along a drive on your left. To complete the walk, ignore the church access drive and within a few yards turn right through a kissing gate. Follow a headland path through to another lane, go right for a few yards to a T-junction and then left.

❼ After 220 yards go left over a stile, then half-right across a field to another stile beneath a large oak tree, and across a field corner to a third stile. Walk round the right-hand edge of the field beyond until after about 150 yards you can go right on a clear path through a wooded dip. On the other side of the wood, go through a kissing gate and left, beside the wood at first, then obliquely up a grassy slope, passing under power lines to find a stile. Keep to the left-hand edge of the next field until you can enter an enclosed tarmac twitten (passageway) between houses. At a lane, turn left, cross another lane and go ahead to reach Barcombe High Street next to the Royal Oak pub.

FLETCHING

Length: 4¼ miles

<table>
<tr>
<td>

Getting there: The best access to Fletching is from the A272 road at Piltdown, about 3 miles west of Uckfield. It is also possible to reach the village from the A22 at Nutley or the A275 north of Sheffield Park.

</td>
<td>

Parking: There is a free village car park to the east of the High Street opposite the Griffin Inn.

</td>
<td>

Maps: OS Landranger - Brighton and the Downs 198 or OS Explorer - Ashdown Forest 18 (GR 429235).

</td>
</tr>
</table>

Fletching occupies a relatively isolated position well away from main roads, overlooking the valley of the upper river Ouse and surrounded by fertile farmland. It is a neat and compact village with few modern additions and is a regular contender for the annual best kept village trophy. It consists essentially of a single main street lined by houses of exceptional quality, many of them timber fronted. At the southern end of the village street, opposite the church, a castellated gateway provides private access into Sheffield Park.

The sandstone church, notable for its lofty spire, contains the Sheffield family mausoleum built by the first Earl of

---

FOOD and DRINK

Fletching supports two exceptional pubs, both offering excellent food. The 16th century Griffin Inn has a particularly classy menu, normally including a number of fresh fish dishes (Tel: 01825 722890).

Sheffield in the 18th century and includes the tomb of the historian Edward Gibbon who was a friend of the family. The church also contains two exceptional 14th century brasses of a knight and his lady. Another brass depicts Peter Denot, a local man who took part in Jack Cade's revolt in 1450. Simon de Montfort camped at Fletching in 1264 on the night before the Battle of Lewes when he defeated the forces of Henry III and his son, later Edward I.

This relaxing walk follows a very gently undulating route along field paths and quiet lanes to the north of the village. Although never rising more than a few feet above sea level, it offers good views southwards across the Ouse valley to the distant South Downs.

THE WALK

❶ From the car park, return to the High Street and turn right to head northwards out of the village. After about 300 yards, opposite the entrance to Atherall's Farm, turn left through a white gate and follow a farm track gently down into a valley. After another 500 yards, from the point where the track ends at a gate, veer slightly left across a field to another gate. Follow the

The sandstone church at Fletching.

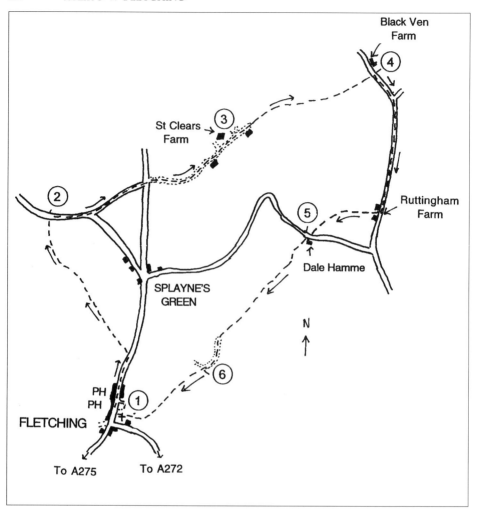

right-hand edge of the field beyond until you can bear right on a track through into the next field. Head out across the middle of this field to join a road through a gate.

❷ Turn right and, at a road junction, fork left along a narrower lane. At the next road junction, turn left and after 20 yards go right along a roughly metalled access drive. Follow this drive until, after 600 yards and with the buildings of St Clears Farm over to your left, you should fork right, still on a clear access drive.

❸ Ignore a left fork, cross a stream and pass in front of a cottage on your right to reach a gate. Cross a meadow to a makeshift stile and go forward on an unfenced track, walking parallel to woodland on your right. Beyond the wood, go ahead across the field to a stile and on through a prominent gap. Now veer very slightly left across a large field to join a lane over a stile beside a gate a few yards to the right of Black Ven Farm.

❹ Turn right and follow the lane for ½ mile. A few yards past the entrance to the farm shop at Deer View Farm, go right along a gravel access which quickly narrows to a path beside a wall. Where this ends, go over awkward fixed railings with a stable on your right, and forward along a track. After 30 yards, where the track divides, fork right. Beyond a stile beside a gate, bear left round a left-hand field edge until you can go left over another stile. Cross a field to join a lane over a third stile opposite Dale Hamme, a fine timber-fronted house with a roof of Horsham stone.

❺ Go right for 5 yards, left along a concrete drive to a gate and then down across a field to a footbridge. Beyond the bridge, bear half-right across a water meadow to the next stile, then go forward across two fields where the path is normally marked out through any seasonal crop. Go over another footbridge in a wooded dip and follow the direction of a waymark across the field beyond to enter and follow a hedged track.

❻ After a little over 200 yards, go left over a stile. From this point cross the first field with the spire of Fletching church as a marker, and then a second field, aiming a little to the right of a row of grain silos. Go through a kissing gate and bear left through the churchyard back into the village.

RODMELL

Length: 4 or 7¼ miles

Getting there: Rodmell lies on what was once the main road linking Lewes and Newhaven on the west side of the Ouse valley, declassified following the upgrading of the A26 on the other side of the river. The village street, a cul-de-sac, leaves the through road by the Abergavenny Arms pub.

Parking: There is a good National Trust car park at the far end of the village street (GR 420063), though its use is restricted to visitors to Monk's House on days of opening. On other days parking is permitted at the discretion of the Trust. Parking is also possible in places beside the village street.

Maps: OS Landranger - Brighton and the Downs 198 or OS Explorer - South Downs Way, Steyning to Newhaven 17 (GR 420063).

Rodmell is a quiet and completely unspoilt village, standing in isolation on slightly raised ground overlooking the drained marshes of the Ouse valley known as the Brooks. Until about 1790 when the river embankment was constructed, the Ouse estuary extended to the village allowing direct access to the sea at high tide. Much of the long village street is lined by flint walls and flint is the main building material for many of the houses. The Norman church has been less heavily restored than most of this age. The only approach to it is through the village school playground.

The start of this varied walk takes you through the village and up to the top of the Downs escarpment. From here the longer version follows a loop which extends deeply into the undulating dip slope of the Downs. Both walks then rejoin to follow a new section of the South Downs Way which takes you down to the village of Southease where the church, beautifully set beside the village green, contains wall paintings uncovered in the 1930s. The church has an attractive round tower, one of only three in Sussex. They are all to be found in the Ouse valley, the other two being at Piddinghoe and St Anne's, Lewes. The three churches stand in a straight line, a fact of significance to ley-line enthusiasts. The return route from Southease follows the raised bank of the river Ouse before crossing the Brooks back to Rodmell.

The Walk

❶ From the entrance to the car park turn left and walk back along the village street.

One of the charming cottages to be found in Rodmell.

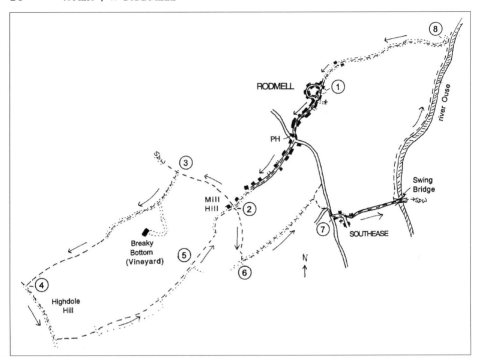

Go straight across the Lewes to Newhaven road and ahead up the No Through Road opposite.

❷ For the longer walk, at the top of the hill in front of the gateway to a house called Mill Hill turn right along the South Downs Way, signposted as a public bridleway to Front Hill. The path is enclosed at first but then opens out to give wide views to the right across the Ouse valley to Mount Caburn.

Those taking the shorter walk, turn left along the Way and follow the directions given below at point 5.

❸ After 600 yards, turn left along an access drive laid with concrete strips. At the entrance gate to Breaky Bottom

Vineyard, fork right along a chalk and flint track which drops down into a sheltered valley with the vineyard, protected by shelter belts of trees, nestling down in a hollow on your left. From the bottom of the hill maintain the same direction on a grassy track, along a headland at first, then between two fields to a stile. A faint path now continues across the middle of a field, up and over the skyline to join a track through a weighted bridle gate, with a new view opening out ahead towards the coast at Saltdean.

❹ Turn left along the track. After a little over 500 yards go left through a bridle gate with a yellow arrow on it indicating the start of a footpath. A faint path leads to another bridle gate. Carry on across open

---

PLACES of INTEREST

Monk's House, near the start of the walk, is a converted farmhouse now famous as the former home of the writers Virginia and Leonard Woolf, who lived there from 1919. In 1941 Virginia committed suicide by drowning in the river Ouse, but Leonard stayed on there until his death in 1969. The house and garden, administered by the National Trust, are now open to the public from April to the end of October, Wednesday and Saturday only, 2 pm to 5.30 pm.

The nearby county town of **Lewes**, a few miles upstream along the Ouse valley, is well worth a visit while in the area. Apart from the castle, built soon after the Norman Conquest, and the 16th century timber-framed Anne of Cleves House, there are many other fine buildings along the High Street and lining the narrow cobbled streets and 'twittens' (the Sussex term for a narrow passageway).

---

downland walking parallel to but about 80 yards away from a fence on your right. Path and fence eventually converge at a bridle gate in a crossing fence.

❺ After a few more yards, where the fence on your right turns away to your right, you should go ahead veering very slightly left and dropping down the end of a ridge. Towards the bottom of the hill, go through a bridle gate and forward on a clear path with a fence on your right. Follow this path as it veers left then right up to the top of Mill Hill where you will find yourself back at point 2. Just short of the gate leading out to the road at the top of Mill Hill you should turn right on an unfenced track, a

newly opened section of the South Downs Way. (Short walk directions also continue here.) The path is well waymarked as it drops down the end of another ridge to a junction with a farm access track in Cricketing Bottom.

❻ Turn left and follow this track along the floor of the valley. After a little over ½ mile the track veers left up to the road and provides a direct short cut back to Rodmell. However, to complete the full walk you should turn right on a fenced track which soon veers left over a small hill and out to join the Telscombe road. Turn left out to the junction with the Lewes to Newhaven road where you go right.

❼ Shortly, turn left along the No Through Road to Southease village. Follow it past Southease church and village green on your right and on for just under ¼ mile to reach a swing bridge over the river Ouse. Do not cross the bridge. Instead, turn left along the nearside river bank, signposted as a footpath to Lewes. Follow the raised river bank for about a mile.

❽ On reaching a stile with a blue arrow on it pointing to the left, turn left along a roughly metalled track. This takes you back after another ⅔ mile to Rodmell where it joins the village street next to the car park entrance.

FIRLE

Length: 5 or 9 miles

<table>
<tr><td>Getting there: Firle is signposted southwards from the A27 Lewes to Eastbourne road about 4 miles from Lewes. At a junction, go ahead along a No Through Road. At a second junction fork left, signposted to Firle Village.</td><td>Parking: The village car park is signposted to the left of the lane before you get to the village. Roadside parking is discouraged in the village itself.</td><td>Maps: OS Landranger - Brighton and the Downs 198 and Eastbourne and Hastings 199 or OS Explorer-South Downs Way, Newhaven to Eastbourne 16. (GR 469074).</td></tr>
</table>

The village of Firle is still labelled as West Firle on OS maps, though the 'West' was officially dropped as far back as 1971 (East Firle disappeared a lot earlier). By whatever name, it is a delightful place, nestling, like so many downland villages, on the spring line beneath the northern escarpment. It is almost completely unspoilt with very little recent building. To the west is Firle Place, seat of the Gage family since 1496. The 500th anniversary of the inheritance of manorial rights by the Gages is commemorated in an excellent little booklet, *Firle - 500 years a village*,

---

FOOD and DRINK

The 300 year old Ram Inn at Firle was once a busy coaching inn, one of four in or near the village until the nearby turnpike road was superseded in 1812. It still attracts visitors from far afield. Though it has gone a bit up-market in recent years, the pub still has the feel of a good village local with a plain 'unimproved' interior. The beer is excellent and the home-cooked food includes a number of interesting variations on standard pub fare (Tel: 01273 858222). There is also a restaurant and tea room at Firle Place.

---

obtainable from the village shop, a notable survival for such a small community. The present house is the result of extensive re-modelling and restoration early in the 17th century, when the fine Georgian stone front was created. The church dates from the 14th and 15th centuries and contains a number of monuments to members of the Gage family, including a window designed by John Piper in 1985 and some exceptional brasses.

The walk offers short or long options through exhilarating countryside. Both circuits climb steeply to the top of the Downs, where the longer walk breaks away to make a foray deep into the rolling dip slope of the Downs. The walks rejoin and descend the escarpment to return past Charleston Farm House (see 'Places of Interest') and through Firle Park.

THE WALK

❶ Go through a white gate at the far end of the car park and turn right along a track which takes you out to the village street beside the Ram Inn. Turn left and walk through the village. Carry on past the access road to the church on your left, where the road dwindles to a farm track and

heads for the Downs. Follow this track as it veers round to the left with the flint wall surrounding Firle Park on your left.

❷ After 500 yards fork right on a track which follows the left-hand edge of a wide belt of trees, now heading directly for the Downs once again. Beyond a gate, go forward, soon veering left to climb steadily on a terraced path, one of the many so-called 'bostal' paths which are such a notable feature of the Downs escarpment. Follow it up to the top of the Downs. At the top, continue in the same direction across open downland, converging on a fence to your right where you join the South Downs Way beside a waypost.

❸ For the shorter walk you should bear left and follow the South Downs Way over the summit of Firle Beacon and on for almost ½ mile to point 6, where you will pick up the route description for the longer walk.

For the 9 mile walk, turn sharply back to the right from point 3, along the South Downs Way in the other direction, with the radio masts on Beddingham Hill directly ahead of you.

❹ At the point where the Firle Bostal road comes up to the top of the Downs, turn left along the continuation of this road, which becomes a private road to Blackcap Farm but is also a public bridleway. Beyond farm buildings, continue in the same direction on a track which goes over Blackcap Hill and then down into a dry downland valley. Go forward on a narrower path which winds along the floor of this valley (Stump Bottom).

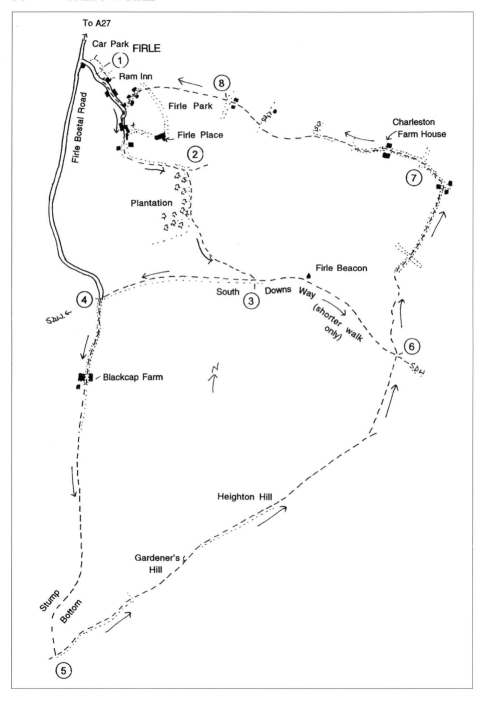

PLACES of INTEREST

Firle Place contains a notable collection of paintings, furniture and porcelain and is open from June until the end of September on Sunday, Wednesday and Thursday (also bank holidays) from 2 pm to 5 pm (Tel: 01273 858335). **Charleston Farm House**, passed towards the end of the walk, became the home of the artists Duncan Grant and Vanessa Bell in 1916. The house contains many examples of their work and that of other members of the 'Bloomsbury Group'. House and garden are open from the end of March to October, Wednesday to Sunday (for more details tel: 01323 811626).

❺ At a T-junction by a waypost, turn sharply back to the left on a narrow headland path which climbs steadily uphill. Beyond a bridle gate, maintain direction across the open ground of the summit of Gardener's Hill and on along the flat top of Heighton Hill, now with a fence on your left. Beyond the next bridle gate the path heads out across a large field where the surface may be disturbed by ploughing. Pass immediately to the right of an isolated patch of scrub and a concrete water trough and climb towards two wayposts on the skyline. At the second waypost, fork half-left to a third post and continue up to join the South Downs Way through a gate and on past another post marking the start of the path down the scarp slope.

❻ If you are arriving at this point on the shorter walk, you will come to a point where the longer route rejoins through a gate on your right. You should turn left past

The path followed on the Downs.

the above-mentioned waypost a few yards off the path on the left. Both routes now follow another fine bostal path from this post obliquely left down to the foot of the Downs, through a gate and onward, passing to the right of a block of woodland. Go straight across a track (the old turnpike road) and ahead along a compressed chalk track. At Tilton Farm, go between buildings to a junction of tracks where you turn left along a concrete drive.

❼ After about 200 yards turn left again and walk up the drive to Charleston Farm House. Beyond the buildings, continue on a rough farm track to a gate and on along the left-hand edge of a field with Firle

Tower directly ahead. About 30 yards short of the field corner go left through a gate and right along a right-hand field edge. Cross a culvert and veer half-left to a gate. Your path then climbs gently across two fields where it is usually marked out through any growing crop. Pass through a belt of trees, descend across a third field and walk between two cottages to join a drive.

❽ Go through the gate opposite and head out across Firle Park. The path is marked by a series of posts leading to a gate and a track which takes you back, past the village spring on your right, into Firle beside the village shop and post office. Turn right back to the start.

HARTFIELD

Length: 3 miles

Getting there: From the A22 at Forest Row about 3 miles south of East Grinstead, follow the B2110. For a more scenic approach from the south, use the B2026 from the northern end of the Uckfield bypass which crosses the top of Ashdown Forest.	Parking: There is no village car park but parking space is marked out along the west side of the High Street.	Maps: OS Landranger - Maidstone and the Weald of Kent 188 or OS Explorer - Ashdown Forest 18 (GR 478357).

Tucked down at the foot of the wooded slopes of Ashdown Forest, the village of Hartfield stands on the southern edge of the valley of the river Medway, no more than a modest stream in these upper reaches. From the busy High Street, the lane leading to the church is lined by attractive cottages.

The church lychgate is overhung by part of the first floor of a timber-framed cottage dating from 1520. The church, like so many in the area, has a fine shingled spire, this one dating from the 15th century.

A.A. Milne, author of the Winnie the Pooh books, lived in the village. The 'Pooh

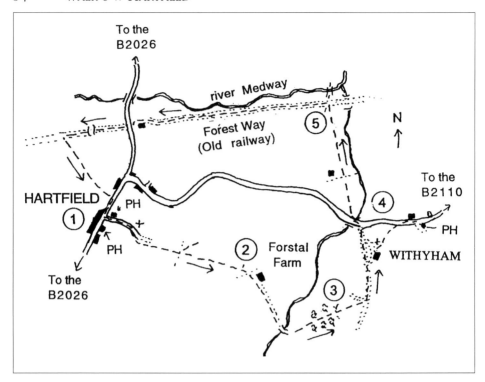

Corner' shop at the southern end of the High Street sells nothing but souvenirs linked with the characters in his books.

The walk crosses fields and parkland to visit the neighbouring hamlet of

---

FOOD and DRINK

There are two good pubs in the village, both freehouses serving a choice of Sussex beers, Harveys from Lewes at the Hay Waggon (Tel: 01892 770252) and King and Barnes from Horsham at the Anchor Inn (Tel: 01892 770424) a few yards up the road. Both offer an extensive food menu. At the Anchor you can go upmarket for quail pate, or back to basics for corned beef hash and fried bread with a wide choice in between. There is a tea room at the southern end of the High Street. The Dorset Arms at Withyham (Tel: 01892 770278) is well placed, just off the main route about half-way round the circuit.

Withyham where the 14th century church was partially destroyed by lightning in 1663. It was rebuilt incorporating the Sackville Chapel, containing memorials to the Sackville and de la Warr families. The second part of the walk uses a section of the Forest Way, a route for walkers and cyclists along the track of the old railway between East Grinstead and Groombridge. The line opened in 1866 and closed exactly 100 years later, a victim of the Beeching axe.

THE WALK

❶ Start the walk along the lane to the church which leaves the High Street between the two pubs. Opposite the church, turn right up steps and over a stile, then left along a field edge. Go over a

PLACES of INTEREST

Several of the sites mentioned in A. A. Milne's Pooh books are within easy reach of the village. **Pooh Sticks Bridge** (GR 470338) is less than a couple of miles away, with car parking to the west of the B2026 at Chuck Hatch. Take your own Pooh Sticks as the area around the bridge has been scoured of all loose twigs. Milne's 'enchanted place on the top of the forest' is accessible from the car park at Wren's Warren, ½ mile further south along the B2026. The site is marked by a commemorative stone, and offers fine views northwards across the Medway valley. It can be found at GR 469322.

concrete bridge into the next field and continue along the left-hand field edge. Once over a stile into a third field, where you have a choice of two waymarked paths across a cultivated area, fork right and follow a trodden path which passes through a line of thinly scattered oak trees and drops down to a gate in the far field corner.

❷ Go forward across the corner of a field to a second gate and then bear left following a headland with a fence on your left, soon skirting to the right of a house and garden. After about 400 yards, bear left across a solid brick bridge. Immediately beyond the bridge you should ignore the obvious track ahead and instead bear half-left across rough pasture where there is a path, faint at first, which soon becomes more obvious as it enters woodland.

❸ On the other side of the wood go over a stile and ahead across parkland to join a

The timber-framed cottage which overhangs the church lychgate.

drive over a stile in the far right-hand field corner. Turn left, immediately ignoring another drive on your left. Follow the drive for 400 yards, passing Withyham church on your right, to join the B2110 and turn left.

(To visit the Dorset Arms pub, avoiding an awkward section of road, walk through the churchyard to find a swing gate behind the church. Drop down across a meadow to reach the B2110 through a second swing gate. Turn right for 100 yards.)

❹ Cross a bridge over a stream and, after a few yards, go right over a stile. Follow the direction of a Wealdway sign across a field to the next stile about 50 yards to the right of a cattle shelter. Cross a second field in the same direction to a gate where you join the Forest Way.

❺ Turn left and follow the old railway for almost a mile, skirting to the right of the old site of Hartfield station and continuing under a road bridge and on along the track bed. Pass under a second bridge and, after another 200 yards, turn left over a stile and go ahead beside a fence to the next stile. A clear field path takes you back to Hartfield.

ALCISTON

Length: 4½ miles

Getting there: Alciston is signposted along a cul-de-sac to the south of the A27 Lewes to Eastbourne road about half-way between the two towns.	Parking: It is possible to park in various places along the village street. The best place is probably near the church.	Maps: OS Landranger - Eastbourne and Hastings 199 or OS Explorer - South Downs Way, Newhaven to Eastbourne 16 (GR 505056).

Alciston, like Firle (Walk 5), nestles at the foot of the northern escarpment of the Downs, on the spring line where water bubbles up from under the chalk. Small and unspoilt, the village, just far enough from the busy A27 to be insulated from the traffic, spreads out along the village street. There are several thatched houses, a pub and a tiny flint church dating from the 13th century. To the north of the church, in the farmyard, stand the remains of a medieval dovecote. Nearby is a massive and magnificent tithe barn, 170 feet long, built in the 14th century to house the rent in kind collected from local farmers by the priests of Battle Abbey who owned the estate. The barn is still in farm use, though the splendid outer shell now houses modern

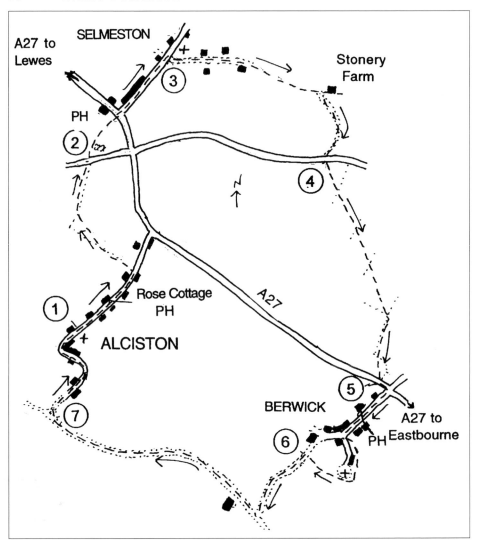

metal containers.

This interesting walk turns away from the Downs to follow good field paths and tracks linking Alciston with two other villages, each with a church and pub, Selmeston and Berwick. The church at Berwick should, in particular, not be missed. The building is of 13th century origin but its most notable feature is the interior, adorned by a series of modern wall paintings by 'Bloomsbury Group' artists Vanessa and Quentin Bell and Duncan Grant, who lived at nearby Charleston Farm House (see Walk 5). They mainly illustrate Biblical scenes but in recognisable Sussex settings. *Christ in Glory*, over the chancel arch, was painted in 1943 and depicts the kneeling figures of a soldier, sailor and airman as well as the Bishop of Chichester and the then vicar of Berwick.

THE WALK

❶ Walk back along the village street towards the A27, passing the Rose Cottage pub on your left. After about 200 yards, almost opposite a house called Hunter's Cottage on your right, you should turn left along a short gravelled access drive to a stile and then follow the right-hand edge of a field. In the field corner, go forward over two stiles and veer half-right across the next field and down to a footbridge in the far field corner. Beyond this bridge, go uphill with a hedge on your right.

Part of the old coach road between Alciston and Berwick.

PLACES of INTEREST

For children, **Drusilla's Zoo Park** is just along the A27 to the east (Tel: 01323 870234) . The nearby village of **Alfriston** in the valley of the Cuckmere river, although overrun by visitors during the summer, is a delight out of season. The giant hill figure of the **Long Man of Wilmington**, of ancient but unknown origin, is etched into the scarp slope of the Downs about 2 miles to the east on the other side of the Cuckmere valley. The best view is obtained from the car park at the far end of Wilmington village street, next to the priory ruins which are no longer open to the public - a great shame.

❷ Join a lane over a stile, go right for 10 yards, then left along a path signposted to Selmeston. It takes you through a small copse and ahead across a field to the A27. The Barley Mow pub is a few yards along the main road to your left but the walk continues along the lane to Selmeston village, opposite.

❸ After almost ¼ mile, just short of Selmeston church, turn right along a metalled drive. Beyond a house it narrows to a fenced path. Ignore a stiled path to the left and after a few yards keep left, through scrub at first and then out in the open, with a fine view southwards to the Downs. Your overgrown path contrasts sharply with the manicured grass on either side, used for producing lawn turf. After another 400 yards, just short of the buildings at Stonery Farm, go through a bridle gate and after 30 yards turn right and follow the access drive from the farm out to a lane.

Selmeston church.

❹ A signposted path starts opposite and takes a well trodden route on an oblique but straight line across several fields, punctuated by stiles and the occasional waymark. In the third and fourth fields you should be gradually converging on minor power lines to your left. Go over a stile, through a gap between two power poles and then veer right, heading directly for the spire of Berwick church along a right-hand field edge. In the field corner, go over a stile and footbridge and ahead across a bumpy field to join the A27 from the left-hand field corner.

❺ Go left for a few yards and then cross the main road and walk along the No Through Road into Berwick village. Follow the lane past the Cricketer's Arms on your right and the small triangular village green and pond on your left. Where the lane divides, fork left and immediately fork left again on a signed path which crosses a stile and keeps to the right-hand edge of a meadow to enter Berwick churchyard through a wicket gate.

Skirt round to the left of the church and leave through another wicket gate. Turn right along a track soon veering right, round behind the church, ignoring the field path ahead. After a few more yards ignore a right fork, keeping ahead along the bridleway, indicated by a blue arrow.

❻ At a T-junction of tracks, turn left and head towards the Downs. After almost 400 yards, at another T-junction, turn right where a red arrow on a post indicates that you are on part of the old coach road, a section of which follows the foot of the Downs between Alfriston and Firle. Until 1812 this was the main road link between Lewes and Eastbourne. Follow this track, passing to the right of New Barn, a typical East Sussex downland feature consisting of a barn surrounded by flint walled enclosures and sheltered by trees.

❼ After another ⅔ mile fork right, keeping to the right of a triangle of rough grass, and follow a flinty track which becomes a metalled lane and can be followed past the tithe barn and back into Alciston.

CHIDDINGLY

Length: 4½ miles

Getting there: Chiddingly is signposted from the A22 Eastbourne to London road at Golden Cross. After a little over ½ mile, at Muddles Green, turn left and you will reach the village after another ½ mile.

Parking: There is a large village car park a few yards along the cul-de-sac to the church which starts beside the Six Bells pub.

Maps: OS Landranger - Eastbourne and Hastings 199 or OS Explorer - South Downs Way, Newhaven to Eastbourne 16 (GR 544142).

Like Wartling (Walk 15), the parish community at Chiddingly is spread over a wide area in a number of small settlements. The focus of the village is still very much at the centre where a handful of houses together with pub, village shop and cricket ground cluster together in the shadow of the soaring 130 foot church spire. The spire is constructed, unusually, from sandstone, one of only three in East Sussex (the other two are at Dallington and Northiam). Inside the church, the main feature is the recently restored monument to Sir John Jefferay who died in 1578. The Jefferay

FOOD and DRINK

The Six Bells is a welcoming unpretentious village pub. It is a freehouse, offering an interesting reasonably priced menu (Tel: 01825 872227). The Gun Inn, which you will come across about a third of the way round the walk, specialises in Sussex dishes made from fresh local ingredients including plaice caught from Newhaven. Try a Sussex Smokie, haddock cooked with wine and mustard, or Sussex fidget pie (pork with apple) (Tel: 01825 872361).

and Gun Hill but now used mainly by walkers. The Wealdway, a long distance walker's route between Gravesend on the Thames estuary and the English Channel at Eastbourne, passes through the village and we use part of it on our walk. The easy circuit of just over 4 miles passes through gentle low Wealden countryside, a patchwork of cultivated fields, copses and tiny streams forming the headwaters of the Cuckmere river.

family lived at Chiddingly Place, parts of which are now incorporated in Place Farm, passed towards the end of the walk.

No less than six public footpaths radiate out from the village centre, originally linking the church with outlying farms and dwellings at Whitesmith, Muddles Green

THE WALK

❶ Start the walk along the No Through Road to the church. A few yards past the church entrance, fork left over a stile where a signpost indicates that you are on part of the Wealdway. Follow the direction of the

The village pub.

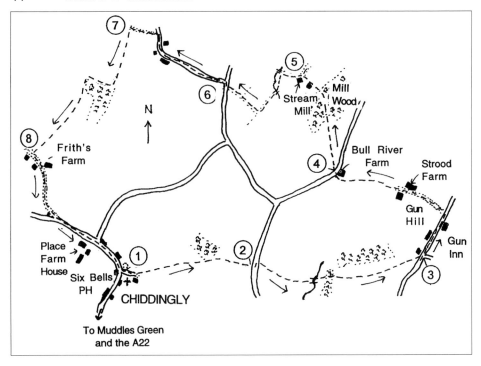

Wealdway sign diagonally across three large fields which often contain an assortment of miniature ponies. Stiles mark the line of the path.

Beyond a stile in the bottom field corner, the path crosses a causeway at the head of a dried up pond and climbs through a belt of woodland. Cross the next field, gradually converging on a line of oak trees on your left, to join a lane in the field corner.

❷ Go left for 30 yards, then right along an enclosed track which becomes a grassy headland path. After about ¼ mile, cross a footbridge, go forward over a meadow, up through trees and ahead in the same direction where a path is usually trodden out through any growing crop. The official route runs roughly parallel to trees on your left to reach a stile in the far left-hand field corner. Go diagonally across the middle of the field beyond to join a lane.

❸ Turn left. After a few yards the Wealdway goes off to the right but you should continue straight ahead, signposted to Horam and Heathfield. Walk past, or better still stop off for a pint at, the Gun Inn and after a few more yards turn left along the concrete drive to Strood Farm. Beyond the farm an unmade track continues through to reach a lane past Bull River Farm House.

❹ Go over the stile opposite, forward to a second stile and then ahead, walking parallel to the fence on your left. Go over a

PLACES of INTEREST

Within reach of Chiddingly, about 6 miles to the west via the A22 and the B2192 is **Bentley Farm** (GR 484159) which offers both a **Wildfowl Reserve** where you can view black swans, flamingoes and many other species and a **Motor Museum** with vintage and veteran vehicles on display. It is open daily during the summer months and at weekends in the winter.

stile in a dip, forward across a field and then through Mill Wood and down beside a field to join a drive. Go forward past the buildings at Stream Mill and on along a clear path.

❺ Shortly, just before a bridge over a stream, look out for a narrow path on the left, marked by a yellow arrow. It winds through a low lying meadow, parallel to a stream on your right, indistinct in places. After about 300 yards, bear right across a footbridge hidden in the hedge. Beyond the bridge go through the gate on your left. Turn right to follow a right-hand field edge until you can go right over a stile and follow the left-hand edge of two fields out to a lane.

❻ Turn right and immediately fork left, signposted to East Hoathly. Follow this lane until, about 50 yards past the entrance to Foxhunt Farm on your right, you should turn left between brick gate posts and along the drive to Clarklye Farm.

❼ After about 200 yards, turn left over a stile. Walk ahead to a second stile and on along a narrow fenced path which tends to be overgrown in places. It turns squarely right and finally plunges through a wooded dip and out to a field edge where you should turn left.

Shortly cross a stile and go ahead with a low bank and fence on your left. Where this fence veers left, go ahead across the field, down to a stile and footbridge and up beside a field to join a drive.

❽ Turn left and follow this drive past the buildings and out to a lane, now back on the Wealdway. Bear left along the lane past Place Farm and back into Chiddingly.

ROTHERFIELD

Length: 5½ miles

Getting there: From the A267 Heathfield to Tunbridge Wells road, take either the B2101 north of Mayfield or the B2111 from Mark Cross. If approaching from the west, follow the B2100 from the A26 Uckfield to Tunbridge Wells road at Crowborough.	Parking: There is no official village car park but roadside parking is possible in various places. There is a useful lay-by along North Street beside the recreation ground at GR 557300.	Maps: OS Landranger - Maidstone and the Weald of Kent 188 or OS Explorer - Ashdown Forest 18 (GR 557297).

Rotherfield (from the Old English 'open land where cattle graze') provided a name for the eastern river Rother which rises to the south of the village at the start of its journey to the sea at Rye. Like so many High Wealden villages, Rotherfield is perched on one of the so called Forest Ridges at a height of over 500 feet above the sea. Many of the houses beside the busy village street also have characteristic High Wealden tile-hung or weatherboarded facings. The 13th century church has stained glass windows designed by Burne-Jones and executed by William Morris.

FOOD and DRINK

There are three pubs within a few yards of one another in the centre of the village. The King's Arms, which has also been known as the 'Rainbow Trout', offers a good range of food (Tel: 01892 853441). Good beer and bar food is also available from the George Inn, just round the corner.

The walk heads south on a lovely route across rolling well wooded countryside. There are several sharp hills and the route finding is not as straightforward as many walks in this book but all the paths used are well maintained and are usually waymarked, and the extra effort is well rewarded by such beautiful surroundings.

THE WALK

❶ Start the walk through a stone archway immediately to the right of the King's Arms pub. An enclosed path takes you through to a lane. Follow the drive opposite. Where the drive ends, go over a stile and turn right along a right-hand field edge. In the field corner, cross a stile and veer half-left downhill across a field to find another stile in the bottom right-hand corner. Cross a stream and keep to the left of the next field. Beyond a stile in the corner, bear right through another belt of woodland. On the other side of the wood climb, parallel to the left-hand field edge, until you can go left over a stile, across a paddock to another stile and then right along a drive to join a lane (Sheriff's Lane).

The pub at the start of the walk.

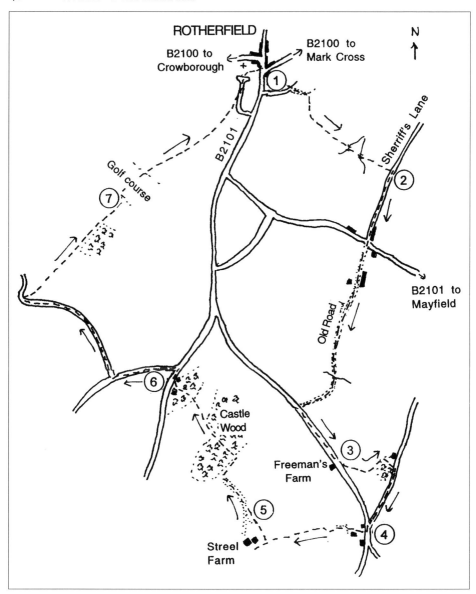

❷ Turn right. At the B2101 go left and almost immediately right along a rough track which skirts to the right of some houses and then narrows to an overgrown path. Further on the path has been badly eroded by four wheel drive vehicles, tempted by its status as an old road. It descends to cross a stream at a ford and climbs to join a lane where you should turn left.

❸ After about 400 yards, just after passing the entrance to Freeman's Farm on your right, you should go left over a stile and follow the direction of a sign half-right across a field to a stile in the corner and then downhill beside a wood. At the bottom field corner, turn right on a track through the wood to join a lane. Turn right.

❹ At a road junction go ahead, signposted to Five Ashes, and after 20 yards go right along the drive to a house called Freemans. Pass to the right of the house and go forward over a lawn to a stile in the right-hand corner of the garden. Drop downhill along a right-hand field edge. At the bottom go through a gate and veer half-left across a field. Go over a stream in a hedge and forward across the field beyond. In the field corner go through a gap to the right of a gate and immediately, where you have a choice of two signed paths, turn sharply back to the right across a field and through a wooden kissing gate.

❺ Go forward for 40 yards, left through a second kissing gate, then right along a roughly metalled drive. At a T-junction, bear round to the right with the main track and after 100 yards go left over railings into Castle Wood. A path winds through the wood to another stile. Now go forward, soon on a concrete drive with the wood on your right. Follow this drive out to a lane.

❻ Turn right and after a few yards go left on a quiet lane which drops down into a valley. At the bottom of the hill turn right, signed to Crowborough. After ½ mile, just beyond the point where the lane veers squarely right, look out for a stile on your right. Follow the direction of an arrow on the stile across a meadow to a gate a few yards to the right of the far left-hand field corner. Keep to the left of the field beyond and go forward over a stile and footbridge. Now follow a headland path, enclosed at first, along the right-hand edge of two fields and over a stile on to a golf course.

❼ Turn left for a few yards then right across several fairways. The path is marked at intervals by inconspicuous posts. Descend to cross a stream and follow a well trodden path with the spire of Rotherfield church now in your sights ahead. Beyond a pond, an enclosed path, which may be muddy, runs behind houses. Join an estate road. Towards the end of this cul-de-sac, fork right. A short enclosed path brings you back into Rotherfield.

EAST DEAN

Length: 6¼ miles

Getting there: Follow the A259 coast road between Seaford and Eastbourne. East Dean is about half-way between the two towns.	Parking: The village car park is signposted southwards from the A259. When full, as it often is during the summer, there is overflow parking nearby.	Maps: OS Landranger - Eastbourne and Hastings 199 or OS Explorer - South Downs Way, Newhaven to Eastbourne 16 (GR 557978).

East Dean, sometimes known as Eastdean, perhaps to distinguish it from the village of the same name in West Sussex, occupies a perfect position in a sheltered dry downland valley opening towards the coast at Birling Gap. Although an extensive new settlement has spread up the valley to the north of the busy coast road, the old village

to the south of the A259 remains unspoilt, overlooking the idyllic village green, an idyll only partially marred by the influx of summer visitors.

The church has a Norman nave and tower and a grave slab from 1300 carved with the arms of the Bardolf family of Birling.

FOOD and DRINK

The Tiger Inn at East Dean enjoys a perfect setting, facing the sheltered village green. The food on offer is of high quality and includes simpler bar snacks such as ploughman's and filled jacket potatoes as well as more substantial fare in the form of a blackboard menu of daily 'specials' (Tel: 01323 423209). You will come to the Birling Gap Hotel about two thirds of the way round the walk. It is a spacious pub but, like the Tiger, gets very busy during the summer. It also operates a coffee shop where you can get a quick snack if time is of the essence (Tel: 01323 423197).

lighthouse built in 1831 was superseded by the present Beachy Head light at the foot of the cliffs in 1902. The route then follows the cliff top path to Birling Gap, where there are steps down to the beach. A steady climb and another switchback route takes you over three of the chalk cliffs known as the Seven Sisters before turning inland across the open grass downland of Crowlink, a 700 acre area of National Trust land where you can walk freely.

THE WALK

This exhilarating walk climbs quickly up on to the Downs and then takes a sharply undulating route across several more dry valleys before climbing to the top of the cliffs at Belle Tout. The old

❶ From the car park, make your way through to the Tiger Inn and the village green. With your back to the pub, walk up across the green and turn left along a lane, almost immediately forking left, signposted

The magnificent view of the Seven Sisters from Belle Tout.

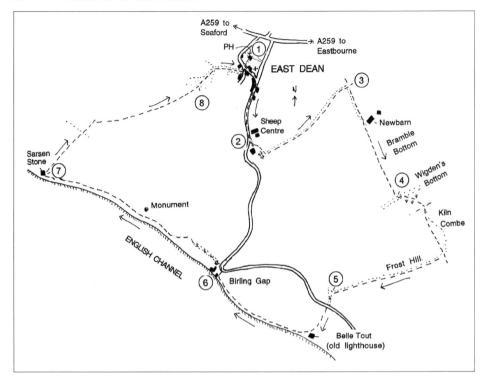

to Birling Gap. Walk past the church on your left, and at a road junction turn right, still on the Birling Gap road.

❷ After a little over ¼ mile, just past the entrance to the Seven Sisters Sheep Centre, fork left along the drive to Birling Manor. After less than 100 yards go left through a bridle gate, forward to a second bridle gate and on along the right-hand lower edge of sloping pasture, skirting to the left of a copse. Beyond a third bridle gate, fork left uphill with a fence on your left. Follow this fence as it climbs and then contours along the side of the hill.

❸ Beyond another bridle gate, turn right and walk uphill, now with a fence on your right. The path crosses a low summit to a bridle gate and then skirts to the right of the buildings at New Barn. The miniature cottage about 100 yards to your left was once in use as a hut for downland shepherds. Follow a fence on your left down into the next valley, Bramble Bottom.

❹ Join a roughly metalled farm track through a gate and turn left for 20 yards through a second gate. Veer half-right on an undefined route across rough pasture and then walk on a much clearer path up through scrub. Beyond the area of scrub, maintain the same direction across the summit of Long Down to a gate.

Go through this gate and drop down into the next valley, Kiln Combe, with a

---

PLACES of INTEREST

The Seven Sisters Sheep Centre, passed on the first leg of the walk, offers demonstrations of various aspects of sheep farming, appropriate enough for this location as for much of the walk you will be passing through sheep pastures. The Sheep Centre is open from March to September, 11 am to 5 pm (Tel: 01323 42330).

The Seven Sisters Country Park, 2 miles to the west of East Dean along the coast road, is a 700 acre area of so called 'heritage coast' downland with open public access and a waymarked park trail. The Park Centre at Exceat contains an exhibition and information desk (Tel: 01323 870280). The Exceat farm complex also houses a cafe and another natural history exhibition, 'The Living World'.

---

hedge and fence on your left. Follow the obvious path up the other side, skirting to the right of a patch of scrub. Follow the fence, still on your left, over another summit to a gate and, once through this gate, turn right to follow a fence on your right with Belle Tout lighthouse directly in front of you.

❺ On reaching a concrete farm drive, turn left. Walk out to a road and follow the path opposite up the steep, scrub covered slope to the old lighthouse. At the top, bear right and follow the cliff path down into Birling Gap with a magnificent view ahead along the line of the Seven Sisters.

❻ Walk through the Birling Gap car park to the road, turn left and immediately fork left on a rough track which passes to the landward side of a toilet block and takes you up on to the cliffs once more. Follow the South Downs Way on an undulating route over the first of the Seven Sisters and down

into Michel Dean. Here there is a memorial with a plaque commemorating the purchase of the area for public use in memory of two brothers killed during World War One.

Carry on over two more of the Seven Sisters and up onto a third where you will come to a seat and another memorial, this time in the form of a sarsen stone. It was erected by the Society of Sussex Downsmen to commemorate the purchase of a further extensive area of open downland at Crowlink for public enjoyment. It is now a public open access area looked after by the National Trust.

❼ At this point, turn right and walk squarely away from the sea along Flagstaff Brow. About 100 yards beyond a swing gate, fork right on a faint path which climbs over the highest point on the immediate skyline and continues, undefined, across open sheep pasture. This is one of the few areas on the Downs today which gives you a feel of what they must have been like in the early years of this century.

❽ After over ½ mile, go over a stile beside a gate and forward for 100 yards to a fence where you should bear right. Now follow this fence downhill, keeping it on your left. It leads to a point where two flint walls join at right angles and where there are steps over both walls. Go over the steps on the right and then continue downhill with the wall on your left. In the field corner, go through a metal gate and follow a narrow enclosed path down between gardens to join a lane. Turn left and walk back to the village green at East Dean.

JEVINGTON

Length: 6 miles

Getting there: Jevington is on the unclassified road which links the A259 coast road at Friston with the A27 Lewes to Eastbourne road at Polegate. The village is about half-way between the two main roads.	Parking: There is a small public car park at the southern end of the village, signposted to the west of the road.	Maps: OS Landranger - Eastbourne and Hastings 199 or OS Explorer - South Downs Way, Newhaven to Eastbourne 16 (GR 562012).

Jevington is ideally situated in the heart of the South Downs, tucked down in a sheltered valley between high hills. The village, consisting mainly of scattered houses beside a single street, lacks a central focus but is a place of great charm.

The church, constructed from flint, is typical of many in the downland area.

Although much restored it has a partly Saxon tower and, inside, a remarkable Saxon sculpture, discovered under the belfry floor in 1875. It has been interpreted as Christ thrusting his sword, shaped like a cross, into the Devil's mouth.

After a steady climb up to the west of the village, the walk passes through part of

FOOD and DRINK

The Eight Bells (Tel: 01323 484442) at the northern end of the village, is a popular walker's pub which offers excellent beer and good home-cooked food including a popular range of pies and quiches. There are tea rooms at the other end of the village, within a few yards of the car park at the start of the walk.

Friston Forest, 2,000 acres of broadleafed woodland first planted in 1926 to protect Eastbourne's water catchment area. It then visits Lullington Heath, a national nature reserve, notable as an example of chalk heath where chalk and acid loving plants thrive together. The final section of the walk climbs to cross a superb area of high open downland with exceptional views.

THE WALK

❶ The walk starts along the car park access road which, just beyond the parking area, narrows to a rough track, signposted as a public bridleway to Westdean. As you climb steadily up out of the valley, pause to look back over the valley to the heights of Combe Hill and Willingdon Hill.

❷ At the top, go ahead across a gallop and into Friston Forest, passing a Forestry Commission notice. Go straight over a forestry road and after another 600 yards fork right, signposted to Charleston Bottom. A track drops obliquely down the side of a wooded valley. On reaching a broad crossing track, bear right, signposted to Long Man.

Lullington Heath nature reserve.

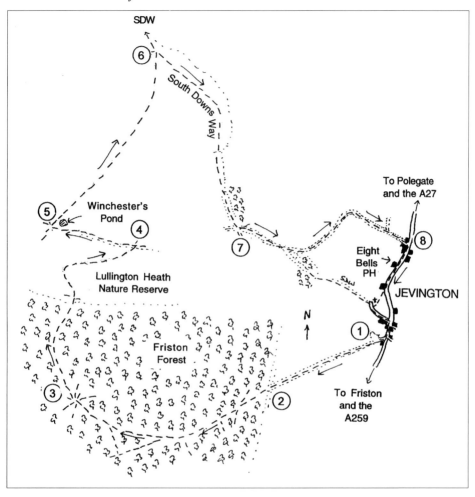

❸ At the bottom of the hill where a number of tracks and rides meet, veer half-right, signed to Lullington Heath Nature Reserve. A broad grassy ride winds along the floor of the valley. Ignore a right fork and after ½ mile go through a gate, passing a notice indicating that you are entering the nature reserve. Follow the main path ahead as it winds through scrub, still along the valley floor. You may come across a small herd of horses which are used as grazing animals within the reserve.

❹ After about 700 yards, go through another gate and turn sharply back to the left on a chalk and flint track which climbs steadily out of the valley. Just before reaching the top of the hill you can seek out Winchester's Pond, hidden behind scrub on your right. This restored dewpond provides a haven for insect and pond life, notably dragonflies.

❺ After a few more yards, where the track levels out beside another nature reserve notice, turn right, signposted once again to the Long Man. A clear track soon leaves the nature reserve and crosses high open downland, following a gently rising ridge. To your left, the village of Alfriston comes into view down in the Cuckmere valley with the hills rising beyond to the distinctive summit of Firle Beacon (see Walk 5). Where the track curves away to the right, go forward through a weighted bridle gate and on across open downland, walking parallel to the fence on your left, with a dry downland combe dropping steeply down beyond.

❻ Where this fence on your left begins to curve away to the left round the head of the combe, you should turn sharply back to the

right past an isolated post indicating that you are now on the South Downs Way. Now follows an exhilarating walk across high open pasture downland with exceptional views, an all too rare experience on the Sussex Downs today. There are few features to guide you but you should be walking roughly parallel to a line of gorse and a fence away to your left. After a little over ½ mile, go through a bridle gate and converge on an area of scrub to the left, soon entering an enclosed path.

❼ At a junction with a chalk and flint track, turn left, dropping downhill. Where the track divides, you have a choice. For a direct route back to the start, fork right and follow the South Downs Way down past the church and out to the road. Alternatively, if you have your sights set on the pub, fork left along an enclosed path which takes you down to a lane at the northern edge of Jevington.

❽ Turn right, and about 150 yards past the Eight Bells pub fork right along a path bordered by a wooden fence which takes you to Jevington churchyard. It is entered through a centrally pivoted tapsell gate, designed to assist access for coffins and provide a resting point for the bearers. Walk through the churchyard and turn left down the lane from the church, rejoining the direct route. Turn right along the lane for the short distance back to the car park.

FRANT

Length: 3 miles

Getting there: Frant is on the A267 Tunbridge Wells to Eastbourne road about 3 miles south of Tunbridge Wells.	**Parking:** There is reasonable roadside parking available round the village green or along the High Street.	**Maps:** OS Landranger - Maidstone and the Weald of Kent 188 or OS Explorer - Ashdown Forest 18 (GR 590354).

Frant can be found in the far north of the county, within a mile or so of the boundary with Kent. The village is situated at over 500 feet above sea level in an area of the High Weald characterised by extensive woods and parkland, including the once flourishing estates of Eridge (see 'Places of Interest'), Bayham and Groombridge. The short High Street heads north from the large village green to the church and the George Inn.

A striking hexagonal lych gate leads into the large and atmospheric churchyard. The church, restored in 1821, contains a memorial tablet to Colonel John By, the founder of Bytown, later renamed as Ottawa. He is buried in the churchyard and lived at nearby Shernfold Park.

FOOD and DRINK

There are two pubs in Frant, both noted for the quality and choice of beer available. The George Inn, next to the church offers a good range of home-cooked food (Tel: 01892 750350). The food menu at the Abergavenny Arms on the main road includes some interesting pies such as pork and stilton as well as a variety of bar snacks such as filled baguettes and jacket potatoes (Tel: 01892 750233).

The walk is a short and easy one, almost entirely through woods and open parkland to the east of the village. It starts through Frant churchyard before crossing open ground with wide views northwards into Kent. Beyond Ely Grange it drops down through mixed woodland. After a short stretch of busy road, a useful recently created public path takes us back up through more woods. The return route to Frant crosses high ground with more fine views, this time southwards over rolling parkland.

THE WALK

❶ Start the walk through the main entrance to the churchyard, bearing right round the right-hand side of the church. At the far end of the churchyard, go ahead beside a field with a view across the valley towards Tunbridge Wells. In the field corner go ahead through a kissing gate, forward for 30 yards, then right over a stile to follow a pleasant level grassy path which contours along the gentle slope.

Frant village green.

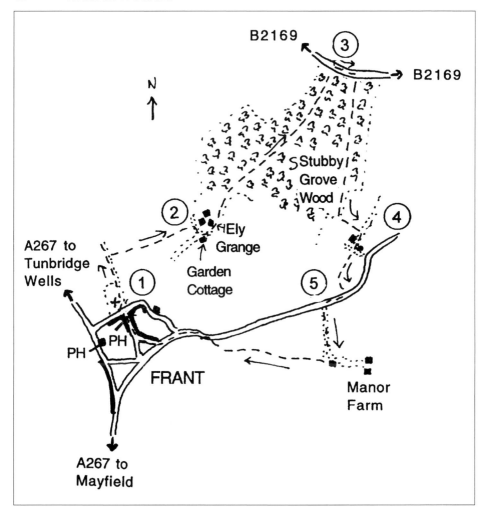

❷ After about ¼ mile, join a metalled drive over a stile. Turn right for 30 yards and then, at a junction with another drive in front of Garden Cottage, go left. After another 30 yards, go left again through a gate and follow a faint grassy track with a high perimeter fence on your left. Follow fence and track to a stile by a gate then continue along a pleasant woodland path for almost 600 yards out to join the B2169 road.

❸ Turn right beside this busy road, taking care as there is no verge. After about 150 yards, opposite the entrance to a house called Brookfield on your left, turn right over a stile next to a double gate. Now follow a clear path up through Stubbygrove Wood, ignoring all side and crossing paths. After leaving the wood, go ahead along the right-hand edge of a field with good views on your left, northwards into Kent.

PLACES of INTEREST

From a small car park opposite the Abergavenny Arms you can enjoy a short circular walk, established under the Countryside Stewardship Scheme, through **Eridge Old Park**. This is one of the largest deer parks in England, which until fairly recently contained the oldest herd of fallow deer in Sussex. The park is now being restored by scrub clearance and tree planting. **Groombridge Place**, about 4 miles to the west, is a brick manor house dating from the Restoration period. The house is not open to the public but you can explore a remarkable collection of exotic small gardens, including a Japanese garden, a restored Victorian kitchen garden and the Drunken Garden, featuring inebriated topiary. The gardens are open from 10 am to dusk (Tel: 01892 863999).

❹ Join a drive and turn right to walk between buildings. At a T-junction with a concrete drive, go straight ahead over a stile and along a redundant tarmac drive which is now reverting to grass. Just short of a gate, turn left over a stile. An enclosed path takes you out to a road where you should turn right.

❺ After about 100 yards go left through the imposing brick gateway to Manor Farm. Follow the drive until, about 100 yards before the farm, you can fork right along a gravel drive. Very shortly, go over a stile in the hedge on your right. There is a notice at this point exhorting you to 'follow the fence'. This is misleading as the official path heads straight out across parkland. Go over a stile in a post and rail fence and on in the same direction across another field to a second stile. A path continues along the top of a slope and out to join a lane. Turn left back into Frant.

MAYFIELD

Length: 4 miles

Getting there: Mayfield is accessible from the A267 Eastbourne to Tunbridge Wells road, about 5 miles north of Heathfield. The village is signposted from the bypass.	Parking: The village car park is signposted from the High Street, down a narrow lane.	Maps: OS Landranger - Eastbourne and Hastings 199 or OS Explorer - Ashdown Forest 18 (GR 587269).

Like Frant (Walk 12), the delightful village of Mayfield is magnificently placed, almost 500 feet above sea level on the end of a sandstone ridge. The long High Street is lined by many attractive old timber and stone buildings, some dating back to the 15th century. The village owed its original prosperity to a position at the centre of the Wealden iron-smelting industry. The 'Mayfield Cannon' on display beside the village street and the iron tomb slabs in the church are reminders of this industrial past.

The church of St Dunstan, Archbishop of Canterbury during the 8th century, dates from 1410, following the destruction by fire of an earlier building. Nearby is the Old

FOOD and DRINK

You can enjoy a pint as well as bar snack or a full restaurant meal in one of the oldest houses in Mayfield, The Middle House Hotel, a half-timbered building dating from 1575 (Tel: 01435 872146). There are two other pubs, the Carpenter's Arms (Tel: 01435 873294) and the 16th century weatherboarded Rose and Crown in Fletching Street at the northern end of the village (Tel: 01435 872200).

Palace of the Archbishops of Canterbury. It was largely destroyed in the 18th century but stones from the palace were used in other buildings. The Old Palace remains are now part of a school.

Our walk turns its back on the village and drops quickly to take an undulating route across a series of pretty valleys cut by tiny streams which form the headwaters of the river Rother. It is a relatively short round which should allow plenty of time to explore the village itself.

THE WALK

❶ From the entrance to the car park, turn left along a lane and after 50 yards go left again along a narrow path with a 'no cycling' notice. On reaching another lane at a junction, go straight ahead. Where the metalled lane ends, go ahead past a cottage on a well trodden path which descends through a wooded valley, crosses a stream, then climbs again to join a lane. Just before you reach the road, look back for a fine view of Mayfield church.

❷ Bear right along the lane (almost straight ahead). After 500 yards look out for a stile on the left. A stiled path now keeps to the right-hand edge of several fields. At the end of the fourth field, cross a

footbridge and go directly ahead across the corner of a meadow to a gate, then between fences. Go through a wicket gate and forward with a high garden wall on your right. After 30 yards, turn right over a stile and continue beside the garden wall to join the access drive from Moat Mill Farm, a fine old converted oast. Follow this drive until, just after it bears round to the right, you can go over a stile on your right and cross the middle of a field to reach a road.

❸ Go right over a brick bridge and, immediately, left over a stile. A sign points the direction across a field, diverging gradually from the stream on your left, to the next stile in sight. Beyond this stile, bear right through a hole in a hedge and resume your previous direction with this hedge now on your left. Where the hedge ends abruptly, turn right. After 30 yards, go over a stile beside a gate and walk through an orchard with a large house and garden on your left. Join a drive and turn left along a gravel drive which soon passes under a short tunnel beneath the disused railway line which once linked Eastbourne and Tunbridge Wells.

❹ Beyond the tunnel, cross a stile and turn left along a field edge. Go over a culvert into the next field and turn right to follow the right-hand edge of several fields with a stream close by on your right until you can recross the stream, using a substantial footbridge.

❺ Keep to the right of the next field. Cross a concrete drive and keep to the right of a second field also but, after less than 100 yards, go right through a gate. Drop

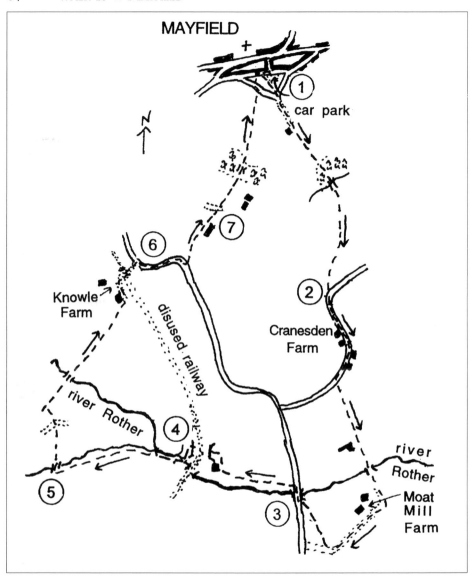

downhill with a hedge on your right, cross a stream, walk through a small wood and then climb steadily along the right-hand edge of two fields. At the top corner of the second field, turn right through a gate. After 30 yards, turn left along a roughly metalled track which skirts to the right of farm buildings with the old railway track bed in a deep wooded cutting on your right. Go through a gate, follow this track round to the right, over the old railway and out to a road.

❻ Turn right and follow the road, taking care as it carries a fair amount of traffic and there are a couple of blind bends. After about 350 yards, turn sharply back to the left over a stile. Walk along the edge of pasture for 20 yards before burrowing into a thicket to find a second stile. Keep to the bottom edge of sloping pasture to a third stile and continue along the right-hand edge of the field beyond to seek out a fourth stile behind a small electricity authority hut.

❼ Cross a drive, climb stone steps and follow park railings ahead with a fine view across the valley to Mayfield. From the field corner a path drops down through a delightful wooded valley and then climbs again. Once out into the open, follow a stiled path ahead across two paddocks and on to enter a narrow enclosed path which brings you to a lane. Turn left and shortly right along a narrow metalled path. At the next lane turn right back to the car park.

The 'Mayfield Cannon'.

WADHURST

Length: 4 miles

Getting there: Wadhurst is most easily reached from the A267 Tunbridge Wells to Eastbourne road about 3 miles south of Tunbridge Wells, using the B2099 road or, if approaching from the south, along the B2100 from Mark Cross.

Parking: The main village car park is signposted from the High Street almost opposite the church, down a road which starts beside the Greyhound Inn.

Maps: OS Landranger - Maidstone and the Weald of Kent 188 or OS Explorer - The Weald 136 (GR 587269).

Although closely encroached upon by the built up area at Durgates and Sparrow's Green, less than a mile away to the north and west, Wadhurst has preserved its identity as a High Wealden village. It is well placed, like Ticehurst (Walk 17) and Mayfield (Walk 13), on a ridge which forms the watershed between the headwater streams of the Medway, draining northwards and eastwards into Kent, and the Eastern Rother which flows through Sussex to the sea near Rye.

FOOD and DRINK

The Greyhound pub, within a few yards of the car park at the start of the walk, offers a popular pub menu during the week (lunch and evenings) and a special weekend carvery on Friday and Saturday evenings, also a good value Sunday roast lunch (Tel: 01892 783224).

Most of the older houses in the village, many of them tiled or weatherboarded, are to be found clustered near the church with its 128 foot shingled spire, surmounting a 12th century tower. The most striking feature inside the church is the collection of 31 iron grave-slabs, cast at various times between 1617 and 1799. They are a reminder that Wadhurst, like Mayfield and Frant (Walk 12), was one of the main centres of the Wealden iron smelting industry.

The walk heads south through typical High Wealden countryside, crossing and recrossing valleys cut by tiny streams, tributaries of the Eastern Rother. It passes through Snape Wood, an area of mixed woodland, managed by the Forestry Commission and uses clear tracks and paths apart from one short section across rough pasture near Snape House.

THE WALK

❶ Return to the High Street, turn left and, just past the White Hart, go left again along Washwell Lane. After about 700 yards,

The churchyard at Wadhurst.

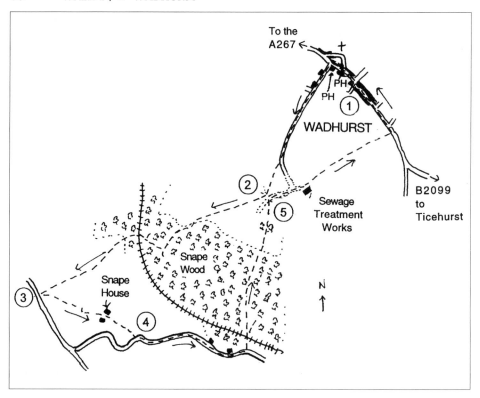

where the lane bends round to the left, go ahead over a stile. Bear left beside a fence for a few yards and then veer half-right over the shoulder of a low hill and down to a stile in the far left-hand field corner.

❷ Go immediately right over a second stile (you can step from one to the other) and follow a narrow path between fence and hedge. Where the enclosed path ends, go forward along a left-hand field edge until you can go left over a stile into Snape Wood. After a few yards, at a path junction, bear right and walk down through the wood. Join a wider forestry track. At the next junction, fork right, and within a few yards right again, following the direction of a yellow arrow along a path which almost doubles back on your previous direction, descending steadily. At another path junction, go left to cross the railway. A fenced path descends to a stream and climbs to leave the wood over a stile. Continue uphill along the right-hand edge of three fields. At the top of the second field there is a good view back across the valley. At the end of the third field you will come to a gate and stile giving access to a lane.

❸ Don't join the lane. Instead, just short of the gate, turn left across an uneven area of rough pasture to join and follow a fence on your right. After about 300 yards, go right through a kissing gate in this fence and follow a much clearer path with a high fence on your right. Go straight across a drive and along the roughly metalled track, opposite. Where the track bends to the left towards buildings, go ahead through a high wooden swing gate and forward, passing to the right of a timber-fronted building surmounted by a clock tower (Snape Farm). Continue between two garden areas to a gate and in the same direction across a field to a lane.

❹ Bear left down the lane and follow it for almost ½ mile as it drops down into a valley. At the bottom, cross a stream and after another 150 yards or so turn left along a clear woodland path. Recross the railway, go straight over a wide forest track and ahead along a narrow path marked by a yellow arrow. Go straight across another forest track and shortly leave the wood and go forward along a well marked path through three fields.

❺ Join a gravel drive and turn right. At a junction with a metalled lane, fork right. At the entrance gate to a sewage treatment works, bear left on a grassy path with a high perimeter fence on your right. Beyond a stile, go ahead uphill, veering slightly left across a field to join and follow a hedge on your left. Follow this hedge up through two fields and out to the B2099 via a short enclosed path. Turn left back into Wadhurst.

WARTLING

Length: 4¾ miles

Getting there: From the A271 Hailsham to Battle road, head south on the unclassified road, signposted to Pevensey, which leaves the A road about half-way between Windmill Hill and Boreham Street. Parking: There is no convenient parking in the village of Wartling.	Take the tiny unclassified road which starts beside the pub (signposted 'Horse Walk') and follow it for a little over ½ mile down on to the levels. There is a convenient parking area just beyond Horse Bridge at GR 669090. The walk can be started from this point.	Maps: OS Landranger - Eastbourne and Hastings 199 or OS Explorer - Hastings and Bexhill 124 (GR 669090).

Wartling occupies a fine position on a low bluff overlooking the extensive 10,000 acres of the reclaimed marshland of Pevensey Levels, once covered by the sea at high tide but now criss-crossed by an elaborate network of drainage ditches. The village was at one time much larger but now the focus of the community within the parish has shifted to Boreham Street, 2 miles to the north. The small church has a pleasant weatherboarded bell tower and inside, a striking modern lectern, carved in

FOOD and DRINK

For such a small village, with no other facilities, it comes as a surprise to find such a substantial pub. The solidly built Lamb Inn in the centre of Wartling should not be confused with another 'Lamb' pub about 2 miles away across Pevensey Levels. It is a freehouse, serving a good range of beers and top quality home-cooked food either in the bar or the separate restaurant. The puddings are particularly impressive (Tel: 01323 832116).

elm in the form of a heron rather than the usual eagle.

From a point about ½ mile from the village, the circuit starts with a short walk beside the wide channel of Waller's Haven. It then climbs to higher ground, looping to the north of Wartling to pass close to the telescope domes of the former Greenwich Royal Observatory. You will also get a good view of Herstmonceux Castle, dating from 1441, one of the first substantial buildings to be constructed in brick in this country. Surrounded by a moat, the interior was stripped in the 18th century in order to enlarge the nearby Herstmonceux Place. The castle was restored in 1911.

THE WALK
❶ Walk back to the west side of Horse Bridge and, immediately, turn right over a stile and follow the bank of the wide Waller's Haven with the water on your right. After about 400 yards, just past the point where the drainage channel makes a sharp turn to the right, follow a signposted

Herstmonceux castle.

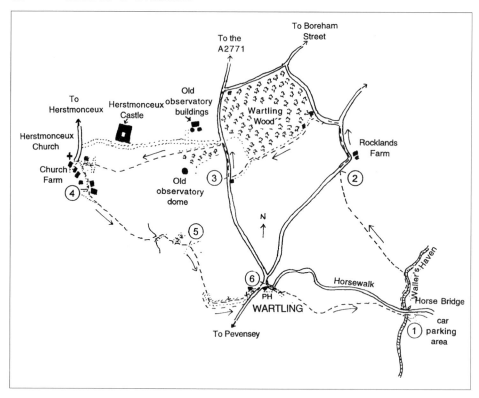

path to the left. Keep to the left of the first field. In the field corner go left over a stile and then right, climbing gently along the right-hand edges of three fields to join a lane.

❷ Turn right, soon passing the entrance to Rocklands Farm on your right. After another 250 yards or so, go left along Jenner's Lane. After another 100 yards, go left through a gap and immediately right along a field edge, signposted as a public footpath to Herstmonceux Castle. It is also part of the 1066 Country Walk, a long distance route linking Pevensey and Rye via Battle and marked at intervals with red discs, which you will now be following as far

as Herstmonceux church.

Follow a generous headland path (a model of how such paths should be maintained but rarely are) round two sides of a field with Wartling Wood soon on your right and a fine view of the South Downs. About 30 yards short of the field corner, fork right along a narrow path into the wood. Bear left along a raised bank to leave the wood and follow a left-hand field edge out to a road.

❸ Turn right and, after a little over 200 yards, go left on a bridleway signed to Herstmonceux church and Pevensey. Now follow a clear, well maintained track westwards for over ½ mile with the domes of the old Observatory (the so-called Equatorial Group) on your right at first and later, when the track crosses open ground, a good view of Herstmonceux Castle. Finally go forward along a metalled drive and just beyond a gate, with Herstmonceux church about 100 yards in front of you, turn left into the entrance to Church Farm House. Immediately fork left on an enclosed path which squeezes between buildings.

❹ Go over two stiles providing access to a field and bear left to follow a hedge on your right through three fields. At the end of the third field, go forward through a gate, over a stile to the left of a second gate and ahead with a drainage ditch on your right. After 100 yards or so, go right over two stiles and ahead along slightly raised ground to the left of the marshes. After about another 100 yards, bear left through trees to a stile and head out across a field where there should be a trodden path through any growing crop.

❺ On the other side of the field go over a plank bridge and stile. Veer slightly right across the next field, down to a culvert and then in the same direction up across a field. An electricity pylon provides a useful marker as there is little sign of a trodden path.

Pass to the right of a pole carrying minor power lines and walk through a wooded dip to a stile. About 30 yards beyond the stile

The old Greenwich observatory 'Equatorial Group'.

PLACES of INTEREST

Herstmonceux Castle is not open to the public but the old observatory buildings have been imaginatively used to house the **Herstmonceux Science Centre**, an exhibition with the emphasis on 'hands on' activities and exhibits, many with an astronomical slant. One of the old Greenwich Observatory telescopes, the Thompson Telescope built in 1896, is on display in its original dome. The Centre is open from the end of March to November, 10 am to 6 pm. There is a cafe selling drinks and snack meals and a shop (Tel: 01323 832731).

the official path enters a hollow way which can get overgrown with nettles. If you have a stick to beat a path, particularly in late summer, you should get through without difficulty. Otherwise there is an unofficial field headland path parallel and to the right. On both routes you finally skirt to the right of a garden to a stile and gate,

respectively, and then turn left past a house and along an access drive to join the lane. Walk up into Wartling village.

❻ Just past the Lamb Inn, turn right along a lane (the one you used to get to the start by car). After a few yards, where the lane bears left, go forward along a roughly metalled access track and very shortly go left over a stile. Follow a sign across fields, crossing two more stiles. Continue on a track along the top of a grassy slope until, after about 150 yards, you can veer left down the slope to a stile and in the same direction across a field.

In the field corner go over a stile, right through a gate and then half-left diagonally across a water meadow to a footbridge. Beyond the bridge, follow a left-hand field edge for a short distance to join the lane at Horse Bridge, back at the start of the walk.

BURWASH

Length: 3¼ miles

Getting there: Burwash is on the A265 Heathfield to Hawkhurst road about 6 miles east of Heathfield.	Parking: There is a large village car park signposted from the main street beside the Bear Inn. Park in one of the long-stay (9 hour) parking bays at the far end of the car park.	Maps: OS Landranger - Eastbourne and Hastings 199 or OS Explorer - The Weald 136. (GR 674247).

Burwash is another village shaped by its past prosperity in the centre of the Wealden iron industry which flourished between the 15th and 17th centuries. It stands high on a ridge separating the valleys of the Eastern Rother to the north and its main tributary, the Dudwell, to the south. The long High Street is partly lined by a raised pavement shaded by a row of pollarded lime trees. The house fronts demonstrate a wide range of Sussex building styles and materials including a rich variety of brickwork, hung tiles and weatherboarding. The most distinguished house, Rampyndene, dates from 1699.

The church, although restored in 1856,

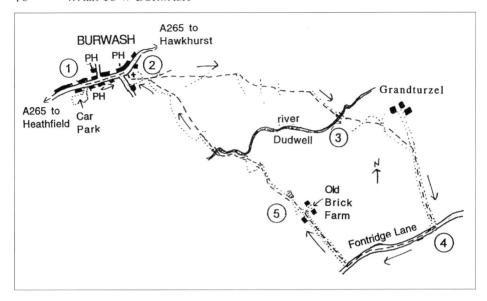

still has a Norman tower with a broach spire, added later. Inside, seek out a 14th century iron grave slab inscribed 'Jhone Collins', one of the earliest ironmasters.

After a stroll along the main village street, the walk cuts through the churchyard and drops gently down to cross and recross the shallow open valley of the river Dudwell with fine views all the way, passing through the countryside described by Rudyard Kipling in *Puck of Pook's Hill* and *Rewards and Fairies*.

THE WALK

❶ Return to the High Street and turn right. At the far end, go right through the main entrance to the churchyard. Walk round behind the church and go ahead to leave the churchyard through a gate and down some stone steps. Where the path divides, go straight ahead, ignoring a right fork (you will come back this way). Within a few yards a fine view opens out on your right across the Dudwell valley. Walk on past a well placed wooden seat.

❷ Beyond a stile the main path goes straight ahead but you should veer slightly right at an angle of about 15 degrees, dropping obliquely down a grassy slope to find a stile beside a yellow painted post.

A short path through trees takes you to a second stile leading out into a field corner. Walk parallel to the left-hand field edge and go through a gate about 40 yards to the right of the field corner. There is another useful waymark pointing you half-right across the next field dropping down to a gate, this time about 10 yards to the right of the bottom left-hand field corner.

Keep to the left of the next field with woodland on your left until after about 150 yards you can go left over a stile hidden in the hedge on your left. Veer slightly right across the field beyond, climbing gently and skirting to the right of a pond

FOOD and DRINK

There are three pubs in Burwash. The Bear (Tel: 01435 882540), next to the car park, is the most substantial. The Bell (Tel: 01435 882304) opposite the church is the most colourful, festooned during the summer months with a fine array of hanging baskets. The Rose and Crown is tucked away along a narrow lane to the north of the High Street (Tel: 01435 872200). All offer a good variety of food and excellent beer. There are also tea rooms at Bateman's (see Places of Interest) and in the High Street.

substantial bridge over the river Dudwell.

❸ The path across the next two fields has in recent seasons been mown out by the farmer. At the end of the second field, descend a grassy bank and bear right along a signed bridleway marked by yellow posts. It soon joins a metalled drive which you can follow out for 550 yards to join Fontridge Lane.

❹ Turn right and follow this quiet lane for almost ½ mile. Turn right along the drive to Old Brick Farm which drops down across open parkland. Follow this drive between buildings where the footpath is clearly marked through a double gate on your left and on along a concrete drive. Where this

surrounded by trees. Go ahead to another stile and then head diagonally down across a large sloping meadow where a path is usually marked out. Go over a stile in the bottom left-hand field corner, forward along a left-hand field edge and on across a

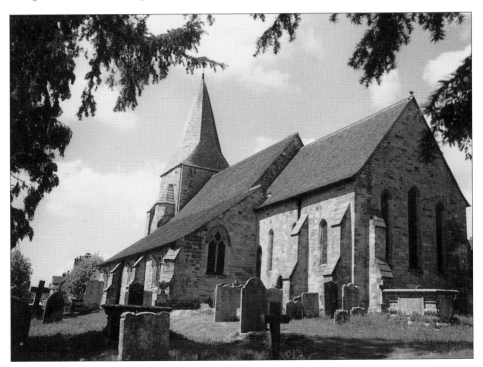

Burwash church with its Norman tower.

PLACES of INTEREST

Bateman's, less than a mile from Burwash, was built for a local ironmaster in 1634, but is more famous as the home of Rudyard Kipling from 1902 and 1936. The impressive stone-built house and garden are now looked after by the National Trust and are open between the end of March and early November, Saturday to Wednesday, 11 am to 5.30 pm (Tel: 01435 882302). At the bottom of the garden a watermill grinds corn on Saturday afternoons when the house is open and also has a water driven turbine, installed by Kipling in 1903 to provide electricity for the house. The house can be reached on foot along a well signed footpath which starts from Burwash village car park.

drive veers left, go ahead across grass to a gate and down along a right-hand field edge with a pond on your right and Burwash church in view on the top of the hill on the other side of the valley.

❺ Follow a fence on your right down to a footbridge over a ditch and then walk half-left across a meadow to cross another footbridge. Keep to the right-hand edge of the next field with the Dudwell stream on your right. After about 150 yards, go right over the Dudwell and ahead along a left-hand field edge, commencing the climb out of the valley.

About 50 yards short of the field corner, go left over a stile and bear right through trees and out into a field. Head straight out across this large field where a path is usually trodden out, aiming for the far left-hand field corner where you will find the next stile. Beyond the stile, fork left along a clear path through a traditional hay meadow which takes you up to Burwash church. Retrace your steps through the churchyard and back along the High Street to the start.

TICEHURST

Length: 7 miles

Getting there: You can find Ticehurst in the far north of the county on the B2099 road which links the A267 Tunbridge Wells to Eastbourne road at Frant with the A21 Tunbridge Wells to Hastings road near Hurst Green.	Parking: There is a good village car park a few yards along Pickforde Lane, to the north of the High Street in the centre of the village. Surprisingly it is often fairly empty even when the village streets are packed with cars. Park in one of the long-stay (9 hour) bays.	Maps: OS Landranger - Maidstone and the Weald of Kent 188 or OS Explorer - The Weald 136 (GR 689302).

Ticehurst is a pleasant village in the far north of the county, within a mile of the Kent border and with a Kentish feel about it. At one time it was a centre for hop growing. Hop fields are now scarce in the area though you will come across several converted oasts on the walk.

Like several other High Wealden villages featured in this book (Wadhurst, Mayfield and Burwash), Ticehurst is situated high on a sandy ridge between two river valleys. To the south the tiny river Lymden is a tributary of the Eastern Rother. To the north the Bewl and Teize rivers

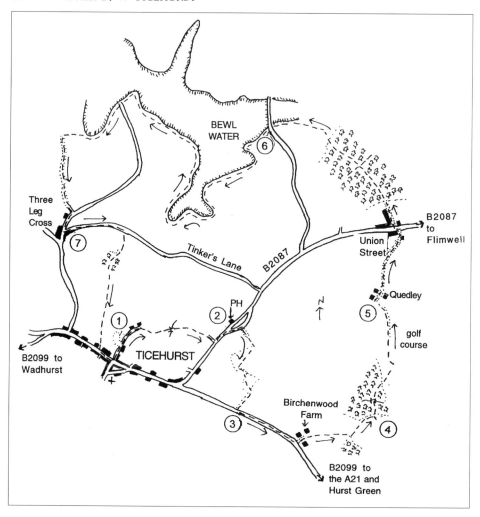

drain into the Medway, though much of the Bewl has now been swallowed up to form Bewl Water. This reservoir covers an area of nearly 800 acres, with a 15 mile shoreline, and when full stores 6,900 million gallons of water. As well as supplying water to a large area of Kent, the reservoir provides a habitat for many species of wildfowl.

This attractive walk crosses rolling well wooded countryside to the east of the village, via Quedley and Union Street, before dropping down to follow a 2 mile section of the Bewl Water perimeter path. Instead of the hop fields of earlier times, we now have a proliferation of golf courses. Our walk bumps into two of them, but takes a short, direct course across the playing area in each case. The return is again through lovely countryside, past Three Leg Cross.

FOOD and DRINK

The 17th century brick and timber Bell Hotel in the centre of the village provides a competitively priced bar menu incorporating local ham and sausages (Tel: 01580 200234). The Bull Inn at Three Leg Cross (Tel: 01580 201289) is within a few yards of the route towards the end of the walk. Though it has served as a pub for only 100 years, it must be one of the oldest houses in the area, incorporating features including timber-framed walls and an open fireplace dating back to 1400 or earlier. The bar with bare floor and beamed ceiling is simply and appropriately furnished and an interesting and fairly adventurous food menu is served in a separate dining area.

THE WALK

❶ The walk starts along Pickforde Lane. From the entrance to the car park, turn your back on the village and head north along the lane. Just short of a bungalow called Pickford Lodge, fork right along a narrow path which continues along the left-hand edge of a meadow. Drop down through a wooded dip and go straight ahead uphill across the field beyond. A clear path continues to join a drive where you should bear right out to the B2087 road and turn left.

❷ Shortly, opposite the car park for the Cherry Tree Inn, fork right and after 100 yards or so, turn right through a gate and along a roughly metalled drive. Just beyond another gate turn squarely right, dropping down across the corner of a golf course and passing to the left of the second tee to find a stile. Beyond this stile, turn left and after

Bewl Water.

a few yards make your way through a gap in a thin hedge. Veer half-right up across a field to the next stile. Once over this stile, turn right and climb fairly steeply with a hedge now on your right. At the top, skirt to the left of a pit to join the B2099 over a stile and turn left.

❸ Follow this road with some care as there is no verge to start with, for a little over ¼ mile until you can turn left along the drive to Birchenwood Farm. After 40 yards, go right over the remains of a stile and along an enclosed path with a high holly hedge on your left and a field of vines on your right. Where the path ends, go right for 20 yards, then left on a clear unfenced track which aims for the corner of a wood. On reaching the wood, veer half-left along a right-hand field edge and, in the field corner, half-right, dropping down with a wood on your left.

❹ After about 150 yards, fork left on a path which descends through the wood and climbs again. On the far side of the wood, follow the direction of a sign across a golf fairway to another sign where you should go left along a tarmac golfer's track. After 100 yards, where this track peels away to your left, go ahead with a hedge on your right to a stile and on along a grassy path.

❺ Where the path ends, go right through the buildings at Quedley and follow an access drive for 550 yards out to the B2087

Scotney Castle.

a right fork. From the far end of the wood, follow a clear trodden path out to a road.

❻ Go through the bridle gate opposite and follow the Bewl Water perimeter path. After almost 2 miles with the water never far away on your right, just beyond a broad causeway bridge turn left, signposted 'Round Bewl Water Walk', ignoring the stile ahead. After less than 100 yards, turn left over a cattle grid and follow a concrete drive for 650 yards out to a lane. Turn right into Three Leg Cross.

❼ After about 200 yards, turn sharply left along Tinker's Lane. (For the Bull Inn, a few yards away, go straight ahead here.) After a little over ¼ mile, just after passing two houses on your left and opposite a stile, also on your left, you should turn right along a grassy headland track. In the field corner, veer right and walk up through open woodland, ignoring a right fork. From the top edge of the wood, go forward with a hedge on your left at first then on your right. A short enclosed path takes you back into the centre of Ticehurst.

PLACES of INTEREST

Within easy reach of Ticehurst via the B2087 and the A21 is **Scotney Castle**, just over the border into Kent. The old moated castle was built in 1370 as a fortified manor house. All that remains today is a 14th century tower and a few rooms dating from the 17th century. The garden which now forms the main attraction for visitors is noted for its rhododendrons and azaleas. It was laid out by Edward Hussey in the early 19th century when he also built the new castle on the hill above and partially dismantled and 'created' the ruin of the old one in its present form. The garden is now looked after by the National Trust and is open from April to October: Wednesday to Friday 11 am to 6 pm; Saturday and Sunday 2 pm to 6 pm (Tel: 01892 891081).

Bedgebury Forest, just off the A21 between Ticehurst and Scotney, is a large wooded area supervised by the Forestry Commission and notable for an extensive Pinetum, transferred from Kew Gardens and planted out in the 1920s. Rare fungi grow here and there is a fine display of rhododendrons and azaleas in the spring. There is a visitor centre (open 10 am to 5 pm during the summer) and for a small charge you are free to wander anywhere in the area or follow the waymarked trail through the Pinetum.

---

at Union Street. Go left for 10 yards and then right along a gravelled drive which, beyond a stile, becomes a woodland path. Go straight over a crossing path and ignore

ROBERTSBRIDGE

Length: 5 miles

Getting there: Robertsbridge is on the A21 Hastings to Tunbridge Wells road about 10 miles north of Hastings.	Parking: There is a small car park with limited long-stay spaces a few yards along Station Road from the village centre. Alternatively the southern end of the High Street is wide enough to allow roadside parking, up the hill from the George Inn.	Maps: OS Landranger - Eastbourne and Hastings 199 or OS Explorer - Hastings and Bexhill 124 (GR 737235).

Although a sizeable community, Robertsbridge has no church and is actually part of Salehurst parish, a much smaller village about a mile to the east. The High Street, now like Mayfield much more peaceful following the construction of a bypass, is rich in timber-fronted cottages, some dating from the 16th century. The village is famous for the manufacture of Gray-Nicolls cricket bats from locally grown willow.

The walk crosses high ground to the south of the village, reaching the A21 at John's Cross, where there is a well placed pub. It continues past the 18th century mansion at Mountfield Court and descends a fine grassy spur with views across the valley of the Glottenham Stream to Darwell Reservoir, before returning along the valley to Robertsbridge.

THE WALK

❶ Start the walk beside the Seven Stars Inn, heading eastwards along Fair Lane. Opposite No 23 on the left, turn right along an access and immediately fork left on a path which skirts to the left of a school playing field. Beyond a stile, turn sharply left across a meadow to cross the bypass, where stiles and ramps are provided.

A trodden path continues to enter Park Wood. Follow a well defined path up through the wood, keeping right at a junction. At a second Y-junction fork right and at a third junction, bear right again for 5 yards to leave the wood at a point from which there is a good view back towards Robertsbridge.

❷ Turn left along the wood edge and after a few yards, at the wood corner, go ahead on an unfenced path which crosses a high grassy plateau with exceptional views. Skirt to the right of more woodland and shortly, at a signposted junction where several tracks meet, turn squarely left, down through the wood. Follow hoof prints across more open ground, leading to a short enclosed woodland track which brings you to Stone Cottage on your right.

❸ Beyond the cottage, where there is a good view to the left across hop fields to Salehurst church, you should turn right along a roughly metalled track. Where it divides keep left, passing to the left of another cottage. Beyond a dip, go ahead uphill across a large field where a path is normally preserved through any growing crop. It brings you out to a lane opposite the white weatherboarded Holly Cottage.

❹ Turn right and, very shortly, go left through a gate and across a field, gradually converging on the hedge to your left. In the field corner you have a choice of two gateways. Go through the one on the left and maintain your previous direction, now gradually diverging from the hedge on your right. Go through the gate to the left of a pond surrounded by trees and ahead, walking parallel to woodland down the hill on your left.

Go through a gap in the hedge just to the right of the top left-hand field corner. Veer half-left across two fields with the remains of a hedge between them to join the A21 road in the far right-hand corner of the second field.

❺ Turn left and after a few yards, opposite the 16th century John's Cross Inn, turn right along a lane which, beyond a brick gateway, becomes a tree lined drive. Where it forks keep left, skirting to the left of the house and garden at Mountfield Court. At a junction with another drive, turn right

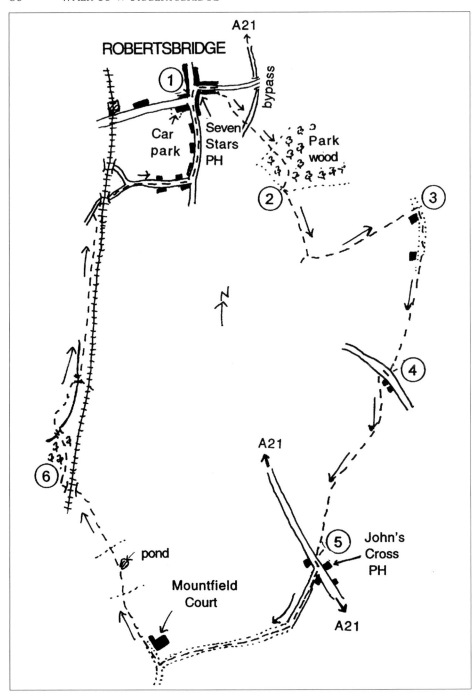

and follow the drive, ignoring a signed path to the left.

Beyond the house and outbuildings the drive becomes a rutted track which soon begins to descend. Go through two gates and ahead down a grassy slope, passing closely to the left of a pond surrounded by trees. Go through another gate and follow a faint track down to the bottom field corner where you should go ahead under the railway and immediately turn right beside the railway fence.

❻ Go ahead on a clear path through a wood, diverging from the railway, then across a meadow to a substantial footbridge over an iron-coloured stream. Beyond the bridge, go right along the right-hand edge of a hop field until you can go right over another footbridge and left, once again beside the railway. Follow the railway fence for almost ½ mile, finally joining a drive. Turn right and follow the drive under the railway. At a junction with a lane turn right back into Robertsbridge.

The view across hop fields to the village of Salehurst.

SEDLESCOMBE

Length: 4 miles

| **Getting there:** From the A21 about 5 miles north of Hastings, fork right along the B2244 (formerly A279). | **Parking:** There is a good village car park a few yards along Brede Lane which is signposted eastwards from the A21 at the northern end of the village green. | **Maps:** OS Landranger - Eastbourne and Hastings 199 or OS Explorer - Hastings and Bexhill 124 (GR 782180). |

Sedlescombe, labelled as Sedlescombe Street on older OS maps, is a regular winner of 'best kept village' awards and is indeed one of the most attractive in Sussex. It spreads along both sides of the B2244 on the gentle northern slope of the valley of the river Brede. Like many High Wealden settlements, Sedlescombe owed its original prosperity to the 16th and 17th century iron-smelting industry and, a little later, the manufacture of gunpowder. Many of the attractive cottages which line the High Street and the village green alongside date from this period. In the middle of the green is a village pump, erected in 1900 by a local benefactor and protected by a sturdy little well house set on eight stone pillars.

The walk descends to follow the river

FOOD and DRINK

The Queen's Head pub occupies a delightful site set back from the main road and looking out on to the village green. It offers basic bar food in the form of sandwiches, plain or toasted and ploughman's (Tel: 01424 870228). On the other side of the road is a small bistro/tea room, providing light lunches, cream teas and a variety of snacks.

Line, a tributary of the Brede, westwards through a lush and fertile valley - so lush and fertile that this may be a walk to avoid during the late summer months when vegetation and growing crops could impede progress. From Whatlington the walk follows quiet lanes and field paths as it cuts across the grain of the land along the undulating northern slope of the Brede valley crossing several tiny streams. On the return it passes Sedlescombe church which stands ½ mile to the north, separated from the main village. It was heavily restored in 1870 but retains a 15th century tower and an interesting limestone font.

THE WALK

❶ From the car park, return to the B2244, turn left and walk down across the village green, beside the road. After 240 yards, just past the Bridge Garage on the right, turn right along a roughly metalled access drive. Just short of a house entrance, fork left on a path which skirts to the left of a house and garden with a children's playground on your left. Beyond a footbridge, fork right along the right-hand edge of a water

The village pub.

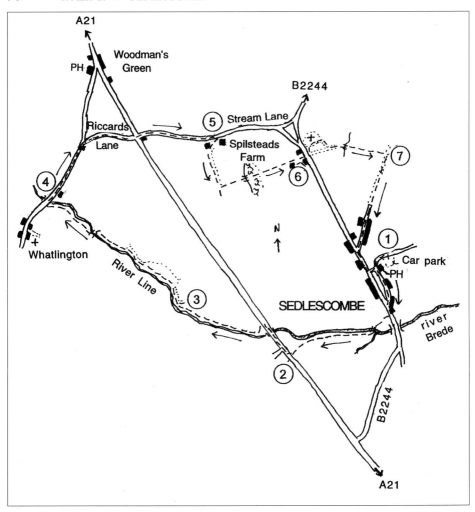

meadow and follow a clear path for about 500 yards to join the A21.

❷ Turn right, ignoring a road turning to your left. Shortly, just past a notice warning of low flying aircraft, turn left through a gap in the hedge and double back to the left inside the hedge on a wide grassy headland path, with a stream (the river Line) hidden in the trees on your left. After a little over

500 yards, you should ignore a footbridge on your left which leads into Petley Wood, now a deer park. Instead, go ahead through a gap into the next field, still along a headland path and ignoring another bridge over the stream on your left.

❸ In the next field corner the path, often overgrown, bears right with trees on either side. After 100 yards the path officially bears left, still beside the stream along the left edge of a field, but may be overgrown and difficult to find. Depending on the time of year and the crop growing in the field, it may be easier to follow the right-hand field edge. Both routes bring you to the far end of the field where it narrows to a point. From here another overgrown but trodden path winds ahead through woodland and out to the corner of a field of vines. Follow the left-hand, lower edge of the vineyard until you can go left over a wide sleeper bridge across the stream. Walk right along a field edge to join a road through a small car park.

❹ From this point Whatlington church is along the road to the left and if you have time is worth a detour, returning the same way. The writer and broadcaster Malcolm Muggeridge is buried in the churchyard. The walk continues to the right along the road. Take care as there is fast traffic and no verge. After about 350 yards, turn right along a much quieter lane (Riccard's Lane). At the A21, go straight ahead along Stream Lane opposite.

❺ After a little over ¼ mile, as the lane descends into a dip, turn right along the short entrance drive to Spilsteads Farm House. After 20 yards, go right through a bridle gate and across a paddock to a second bridle gate. Then go left, soon joining a concrete drive with farm buildings to your right. Go forward for a few yards only along this drive before turning left on a grassy

Whatlington church.

PLACES of INTEREST

There are a number of vineyards in the area, notably **Sedlescombe Organic Vineyard** on the B2244 a mile to the north. Of the 350 vineyards in England only six use organic methods, avoiding all chemical fertilisers and herbicides, and this is one of them. The shop, wine tasting centre and vineyard trail are open from 10 am to 6 pm between April and December, weekends only from 12 noon to 5 pm between January and March (Tel: 01580 830715). The walk passes close to **Leeford Vineyard** at Whatlington where there is a shop open daily from Easter to Christmas and at weekends between January and Easter (Tel: 01424 773183). The world famous **Pestalozzi Children's Village**, an international educational centre, is situated just to the south of Sedlescombe in the grounds of Oaklands, a mansion designed by Decimus Burton in 1834 (neither are open to the public).

---

strip which veers right to a gate.

Now go ahead along a left-hand field edge with a vineyard on your left. In the field corner, go ahead along a wide grassy strip. A few yards beyond a gate, turn left over a stile and walk downhill along the right edge of the field of vines. At the bottom, veer half-left across a meadow to a gate and concrete bridge and climb along the left-hand edge of two fields. Round the top corner and after 5 yards go left over two stiles. The path now squeezes along the left-hand edge of a garden out to join the B2244.

❻ Go left and immediately fork right up the ramped path to the churchyard. Skirt to the right of the church and leave the churchyard through a swing gate. Keep to the right of a field until after 100 yards you can go right over a stile and left downhill along a gravel track. Beyond a stile, an enclosed path drops into a valley. Cross a footbridge and follow a hedge up the other side.

❼ At the top go over a stile and turn right on a clear path along the other side of the hedge. It eventually joins an access drive which takes you back into Sedlescombe.

WINCHELSEA

Length: 5 miles

Getting there: Winchelsea is just off the A259 Hastings to Folkestone road about 9 miles west of Hastings.	Parking: Except at peak holiday times, there is ample roadside parking at various places in the village.	Maps: OS Landranger - Ashford and Romney Marsh 189 or OS Explorer - Romney Marsh 125 (GR 904174).

The ancient Cinque Port of Winchelsea is one of the most beautiful and unspoilt villages in Sussex. After the original town, eroded by the sea, finally succumbed to a storm in 1266, it was partially rebuilt by Edward I in 1292 using a chequer-board street plan. The ancient gateways and the remains of the town walls reveal the grand scale of the unfinished project. The 14th century church, dedicated to St Thomas Becket, would if completed have been one of the largest in Sussex. What remains, the chancel and north and south chapels, is still pretty impressive and contains some fine stained glass. A tree beside the churchyard indicates the place where John Wesley preached his last sermon in 1790 and the walk starts from this spot, marked by a

FOOD and DRINK

The 18th century New Inn in the centre of Winchelsea offers a wide variety of excellent food, cooked on the premises. The inn also provides overnight accommodation (Tel: 01797 226252). There is a village teashop. The Plough at Cock Marling is well placed for food and drink, about half-way round the walk.

commemorative plaque.

From the village, which stands on a high sandstone ridge overlooking the valley of the river Brede, once a sea estuary, the walk drops down to follow the river before climbing the northern slopes of the valley to Cock Marling for a brief glimpse across into the next valley to the north, cut by the Tillingham stream. A couple of the paths on the fairly direct return route to Winchelsea have in the past been damaged by ploughing and obstructed by growing crops but I have asked the County Council to try and ensure that this doesn't happen in future seasons.

THE WALK

❶ From the 'Wesley Tree', with your back to the church, turn right, passing the New Inn on your left. Take the second turning on your left. Cross the main road and follow the drive opposite. Where the metalling ends, go over a stile and forward, skirting to the right of a mound where stood the remains of St Leonard's Mill until it was swept away in the Great Gale of October 1987. From this superb viewpoint across

Pipewell Gate.

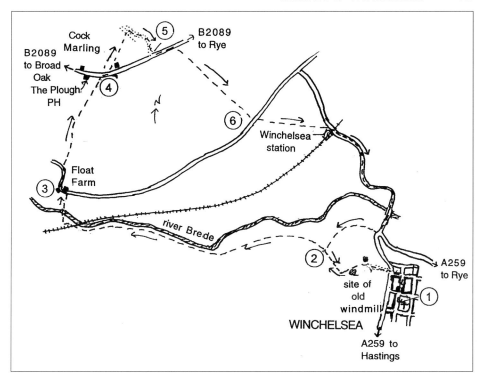

the Brede valley, a grassy hollow way bears right down the hill.

❷ Towards the bottom cross a stile, bear left beside a fence for 100 yards to a second stile and continue with a water filled ditch on your left. Beyond another stile, the path veers left across a large field where there is normally a path through any growing crop. On the other side of this field, join and follow the raised river bank of the river Brede. After ⅔ mile beside the Brede, cross the railway and after another 100 yards, go right over the river and on through two fields to join Winchelsea Lane.

❸ Turn left past an elegantly converted oast and follow the lane round a double

bend. Very shortly, go right through a gate and uphill within another grassy hollow. From a stile at the top of the hill, a marked path continues out to the B2089.

❹ The well placed Plough Inn is a few yards along the road to the left. To continue the walk, turn right and after a few yards turn left along an access drive. Go over a stile to the left of a bungalow and veer half-left across pasture parkland to join a drive through a gate in the far left-hand field corner. Turn left along the drive for 10 yards, go right through a gap and then right again, doubling back on yourself along a parallel drive which you can now follow out to rejoin the B2089. Turn left beside this busy road.

PLACES of INTEREST

The 14th century **Court Hall**, next to Winchelsea church, houses a museum open from April to September, weekdays 10.30 am to 12.30 pm and 2.30 pm to 5.30 pm, Sunday 2.30 pm to 5.30 pm. Less than 3 miles away along the valley and well worth a visit, the hilltop village of **Rye** with its narrow cobbled streets is perhaps the most famous of the Cinque Ports. Like Winchelsea, it once boasted a busy harbour until it was left stranded when the sea retreated.

---

❺ After a little over 200 yards, just past a house on the right, turn right along a woodland path. Beyond the wood, go ahead across the corner of a field to a gate and in the same direction down the hill. This field has in the past been ploughed and planted without any sign of a path through the growing crop. As you begin to drop down, aim for the bottom left-hand field corner where two stiles provide access to Winchelsea Lane.

❻ Turn left and after a few yards go right over a stile and half-left across two fields to rejoin Winchelsea Lane next to Winchelsea railway station. Turn right over the railway and follow the lane. At a junction with the A259, turn right on a path which skirts to the right of a sewage works and brings you to the stile at the foot of the hill below the old windmill site, passed at the start of the walk. Retrace your steps back up to Winchelsea.